WARWICK⁣ TALES OF M⁣ AND MURDER

Betty Smith

COUNTRYSIDE BOOKS
Newbury, Berkshire

First published 2001
© Betty Smith 2001

COUNTRYSIDE BOOKS
3 Catherine Road
Newbury, Berkshire

To view our complete range of books,
please visit us at
www.countrysidebooks.co.uk

ISBN 1 85306 702 4

Designed by Mon Mohan
Produced through MRM Associates Ltd., Reading
Printed by J. W. Arrowsmith Ltd., Bristol

Contents

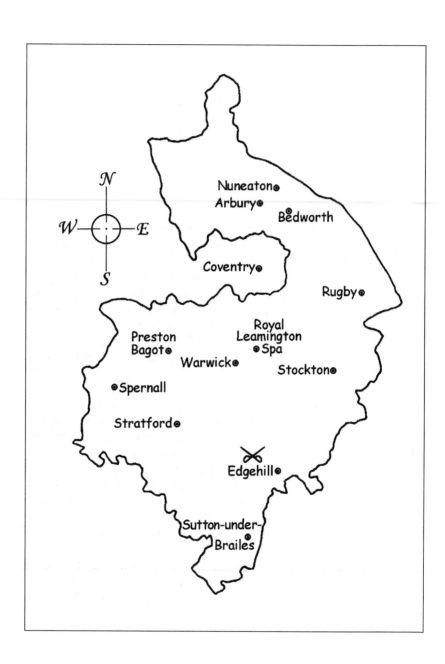

THE MURDER OF
LUCY ASKHAM

THE weekend of 16th March 1913 was a blustery one. A severe storm raged over the defenceless heads of the inhabitants of Nuneaton and the district surrounding it, bringing slates off roofs and littering the streets with the wreckage of fallen chimney pots. When the elements had exhausted themselves, a watery sun revealed something far more sinister than mere storm debris, and the discovery sent a ripple of horror through the town.

Two young men, Joseph Wills and Will Hardy, decided to take the dog for a walk now the storm had abated, and they headed along Leicester Road. They noticed that the deep ditch running alongside the road as it wound its way towards the outskirts of the town was full to overflowing, swollen by the heavy non-stop rain of the night before. Broken twigs and branches were liberally scattered around, and this delighted the little terrier dog who dashed hither and thither as dogs are wont to do. The two young men played with the dog, and larked about a bit, as young men are wont to do. Suddenly the dog dashed off, barking furiously. It paused on the edge of the swollen ditch and barked again with mounting excitement.

Joseph Wills and Will Hardy merely thought that the dog had found something of purely canine interest and they strolled up at a leisurely pace, but they were brought to an abrupt halt at the sight of a woman's body lying, fully dressed, partly submerged in the water-filled ditch. They looked a little closer and noticed pools of blood. The woman had been murdered, for her head was almost severed from her body.

Ashen faced, the two young men raised the alarm; police arrived, and the body was conveyed through the streets to the public mortuary. Residents looking out of their windows at the wreckage of the storm saw in addition the human wreckage of violence and death.

In 1913 police procedures were not nearly as efficient as today; detectives not nearly as knowledgeable. It was not customary to cordon off the whole area around a murder scene, so this was not done. Consequently, the world-and-his-wife converged rapidly upon the spot, alerted by that strange and undefined grapevine that ever carries news and rumours of news. Any real evidence that might have come to light from an expert examination of the ditch and the blood-spattered grass was, therefore, lost. In a matter of minutes, the Sunday boots of the curious had mashed the murder site to a sea of mud.

Not surprisingly, the dead woman's clothing was soaked through. The pools of blood on the grass verge were quite extensive, and there were smaller areas of blood upon the road itself. The clothing was not disarranged in a way that might suggest any sexual assault, nor did it seem as if the dead woman had fought with her assailant.

The victim was identified as Lucy Askham, aged 38. Just under five foot in height, with dark brown hair just beginning to turn grey at the front, hazel eyes and thin features. She hailed originally from Cambridge where her brother still lived, running the family fruit business. For many years Lucy had not conformed but had travelled the roads sharing her life with a man to whom she was not married. In 1913 this was not socially acceptable in any way, and Lucy had little, if anything, to do with her relatives. All the poor woman had on her person when she was lifted from the waterlogged ditch into which her killer had forced her was 2s 4½d, a little bag of potted meat and a small piece of cake.

The inquest into the cause of her death was opened the following week. Dr William Nason said that he had been called to examine the body at 12.45pm on the previous Sunday and gave it as his opinion that the murder took place some twelve hours before, which puts it as late on Saturday night. The death wound, he said, was a clean cut, seven inches in length, inflicted with great force, using a strong, sharp instrument and one firm and powerful stroke. 'The blood must have spurted out', he went on, 'and the killer would have had blood on the right forearm of his clothing.' He told the inquest that only someone very strong could have inflicted such a wound. The dead woman must have been standing up at the time, and death would have been instantaneous. It would have been totally impossible for the victim to have moved at all from the place where she met her death, said Dr Nason.

The most important witness at the inquest was, of course, Lucy Askham's lover, James Williams. The focus of all eyes, he was a tall, gaunt man, with hair turning grey. According to news reports he was visibly moved and broke down more than once, as he explained to the Coroner that he and Lucy Askham had lived together for the past ten years. They were both artists. He was what he called a 'street artist' and moved from place to place, setting out his pictures on pavements in suitable spots. Lucy did sketches and watercolours, usually of local scenes and landscapes, and these she hawked from door to door.

They seem to have made no more than a bare living, but any money they were given was shared between them and they wanted for nothing of importance.

For the past few weeks, they had been living at No. 16 Vicarage Street, Nuneaton, where they had taken an upstairs room in the house of a Mrs Ada Duckett.

'Was it a peaceful life?' asked the Coroner.

'Very peaceful,' James Williams replied. 'I am a peaceful man, and she was a peaceful woman.'

'Why did you not marry her?' was the next question.

Williams explained, in a soft voice, that he was now sorry he had not done so. But he wanted a proper home and a proper marriage. He was a Roman Catholic and he had tried for a long time to persuade Lucy to come into his Church. A register office wedding would not have done for him, James Williams said.

He had perfect trust in Lucy Askham, he continued. There had never been the slightest suspicion of another man in all the years they had been together. Had there been such, he would not have stayed with her. He said that Lucy had taken him to Cambridge once, to visit her brother. He knew that both her parents were dead.

Williams said that on the day of the murder he had gone out, leaving Lucy in their room. He intended walking to Coventry, where he would set his pictures out on the pavement. He told Lucy he would be back before eleven o'clock that evening, and suggested that she should try and return around the same time so that they could have their supper together. He had begged her not to be late, he said. He did not know Lucy's exact plans, but he expected she would go out, knocking on doors to sell her pictures, as she usually did. All this was their normal practice.

He walked to Coventry, a distance of some nine or ten miles, arriving around two o'clock. He set up his patch in Cash's Lane, and did quite well, taking nine shillings. He enquired the time from a passer-by, and realising it was nearly nine o'clock he decided to pack up his pictures and return home. He took a tram to Bedworth, paying a threepenny fare, and from there he walked the rest of the way to Nuneaton. He did not go into any public house, nor did he exchange a word with anyone else on the entire journey, he said.

He got back to 16 Vicarage Street at twenty minutes to eleven and went straight upstairs to the room he and Lucy rented, expecting to find her waiting for him. In fact, he was a bit put out to find she was not there. She had been late before, however, so he did not worry unduly. He lit the fire and put the kettle on, anticipating she would be in very shortly. But she did not return, and around five o'clock in the morning, he went to bed himself.

The following morning, Sunday, he went to pay his landlady 2s 6d he owed her for rent. It was about quarter to twelve, and he grumbled a bit about 'the Missus' not coming home. Mrs Duckett had become a little chatty and remarked that she had heard a woman had been found dead 'along the road'. The woman was, she said, wearing black gloves, according to her gossipy informant. Mrs Duckett knew well it was Lucy's habit to wear black gloves, but at this time she had absolutely no idea that she was talking of her tenant, or of murder. She honestly thought that the unknown woman had been knocked down and killed by a motor vehicle.

At the inquest, Mrs Duckett spoke favourably of her lodgers. They did not owe her money and they were well behaved. Never once had their voices been raised in anger and she had never heard a swear word from either of them. She had never seen Lucy Askham with another man, nor had Lucy had any male visitors. Mrs Duckett had never seen either Lucy or Williams in drink and she only remembered Lucy returning home late on one occasion, and this was because she had missed the last tram and had been forced to walk the whole way.

When Mrs Duckett told James Williams of the woman found dead on Leicester Road, he became uneasy about Lucy's whereabouts and, at the landlady's suggestion, he went down to the police station to tell the officer on duty that his 'Missus' had not returned home. He gave them a bit of a description, and was taken to the mortuary, where he identified the body of the dead woman as that of Lucy Askham.

In the couple of days following, Williams asked the police what he could do to help, but there really was very little they could suggest. So, in a rather amateurish way, he began to pursue his own investigation, closely watched by a reporter from the local newspaper.

Williams, apparently, presented a down-at-heel, depressed appearance as he wandered aimlessly around the town, a most unlikely lover, people said. Tongues wagged, fingers pointed but he chose to ignore, if indeed he saw them at all, those who stared at him.

One day, wandering up Attleborough Road, he noticed a tramp with what seemed to be blood on his sleeve. Williams followed and eventually caught up with him, inviting him into a nearby pub for a drink, planning to ask some questions. The crafty tramp accepted the drink readily enough, but when the questions became pointed, he suddenly made off. Williams, caught unawares, gave chase, but lost his quarry in a maze of back streets and yards. He reported this whole event to the police and they put out a description of the tramp in an effort to trace him.

A further red herring was brought into play when a tramp (perhaps the same one or perhaps not) went into the King William Inn on Coton Road in Nuneaton, and sold the landlord of that hostelry a very good razor in a very good case. The landlord, delighted with his bargain, laid it aside on a shelf. It was not until the news of the murder spread rapidly through the town, and talk of the dead woman's throat being cut with a strong weapon reached the landlord's ears, that he thought he might have, unwittingly, purchased the murder weapon. He reported the matter to the police who made a lot of notes about it but flatly refused to comment more. Indeed, they could not be drawn at all on the matter of tramps.

Later they issued a description of a man, aged 44–45 years, with a slight moustache and a bandaged hand, who had taken a bed in a common lodging house on the night of the murder, but had escaped through a window under cover of darkness. They never got hide nor hair of him!

Much time was wasted checking the evidence of a woman called Florence Rose Long, wife of a Nuneaton street musician. She told friends she actually saw the murder take place, but was too frightened to do anything 'in case the man came back and did for her as well. . .'

The police investigated, as they must always do. She said the murderer was a 'pavement artist who shows his pictures on the streets'. Said she would know him anywhere. But when confronted with a line-up, an identification parade of a dozen men, one of whom was James Williams, she failed to recognise him or anybody else. She said she was on Leicester Road at half past eleven when the deed was done, and waiting for a man whose name she did not know. Three separate witnesses came forward and said she was with them at the time, and not on Leicester Road.

It transpired that this lady was unbalanced. She had been in prison seven times, mostly drunk and disorderly, and had attempted suicide three times (then an offence). Florence's own mother said she could do nothing with her, and nobody should believe a word she uttered. So, Florence Rose Long's evidence was totally discounted.

At the resumed inquest, the jury brought in the only possible verdict. Murder by person or persons unknown. The evidence of Florence Rose Long they referred to as 'purely imaginary'. At that precise moment, the Relieving Officer arrived to take change of Florence and one can only assume she was committed to a mental hospital. It happened so very often in 1913.

So, the unknown killer of poor Lucy Askham remained at large and was never brought to justice. It used to be said, within the police service, 'Find me a motive and I'll find you a murderer', but in this case there does not seem to have been any motive. James Williams had no need to resort to violence; they were not married; neither of them had anything that belonged to the other and he could have simply walked out on Lucy at any time, had he chosen to do so. No money was involved. They had scarcely enough for their daily needs, although this did not seem to bother either of them. There was no sexual motive. Lucy was, according to her photograph, a pleasant enough woman, but not one likely to inflame unbridled passion in any male breast.

Blackmail did not enter into the equation. If she had been doing the blackmailing, she would have had some money somewhere; if somebody was blackmailing her, why kill her and cut off the supply? She would be no use as a source of money if she was dead. There was no evidence that the poor woman had ever had any real money anyway.

The *Nuneaton Chronicle* traced Lucy Askham's last sale. It seems she knocked upon the door of a Mrs Florence Cornell in the village of Sketchley, just over the border in Leicestershire, and the bought a sketch of John Bunyan's cottage for 1/6d. At the time it was raining very heavily and Lucy sheltered in Mrs Cornell's house for a little while. Then she declared she had better get on, because she had to walk back home to Nuneaton. Mrs Cornell said Lucy left about eight o'clock, as far as she could recall. The question therefore remains: what did Lucy Askham do from around eight o'clock when she left Mrs Cornell, until half past eleven, or nearer midnight, when she fell victim to her killer? The spot where her body was found was no more than five miles from Mrs Cornell's house; perhaps an hour's walk, maybe a little more in bad weather. No one else came forward to say they had seen Lucy Askham after she had left Mrs Cornell, and no one (apart from Florence Long) apparently saw her walking along Leicester Road.

So, these secrets went with Lucy to the grave! Nothing more is known. I wonder, however, if any of her watercolours are still around? According to bits and pieces in the local press, Lucy was a talented artist. And did any of James Williams's pictures survive? These too must have been reasonably good if just setting them out upon the pavement could earn him nine shillings in a couple of hours. Way back in 1913, nine shillings was a lot of money.

THE GHOST OF
NEWDIGATE COLLIERY

Right up in the north of Warwickshire we are in George Eliot country, for it was here at Arbury in 1819 that Mary Ann Evans was born, the third child of Robert Evans, land agent to the Newdigate family of Arbury Hall. Then, as we all know, when she grew up Mary Ann 'reinvented' herself, to use the modern jargon; went off to London and became George Eliot. But the scenes of her Warwickshire childhood remained inside her head and heart, and were used many times in her writings.

Here at Arbury, near to Nuneaton and Bedworth, we are on what was once upon a time the Warwickshire coal field. Coal mining is frequently thought of as a comparatively recent industry; the Industrial Revolution and all that! But it is much, much older. There is a history of some eight centuries of coal mining in the Nuneaton area, and it is recorded that in 1275 a licence to mine coal here was granted to one Alexander Compton.

Newdigate Colliery was sunk in 1898, and its first owner was Sir Francis Alexander Newdigate of Arbury Hall. The Newdigates have been in Warwickshire since the time of the first Elizabeth, and elsewhere for much longer than that. They have been connected with coal mining for centuries, and profits from the Griff Colliery, also on the Arbury estate, helped to pay for the rebuilding of the superb Arbury Hall. Because of the name of its founder, Sir Francis, Newdigate Colliery became affectionately known to all and sundry in the locality as 'Frankie's'.

All was not plain sailing, unfortunately; far from it. Fire in the underground workings caused a lot of trouble and production fell

Newdigate colliery, affectionately known locally as 'Frankie's'. (Midland Daily Telegraph)

well short of expectations. A great deal of improvement work was carried out, but it was not until around 1920 that things began to get noticeably better. A decision was taken to mine only the top secton of what was referred to as the Warwickshire Thick seam, and that decision proved to be the right one in this case.

Following the General Strike of 1926, business in the coal industry was brisk, with people all over the country seeking to replenish their much diminished stocks for both domestic and industrial use. Then there was a sharp fall off in demand because somebody discovered you could buy coal cheaper from Poland. From then on, you might say, it was downhill all the way. Some 500 pits closed in the British Isles, and here at Newdigate the workforce was cut from 1,477 in January 1927 down to 942, a loss of around 500 jobs in just one small pit.

They were a cheerful lot at Frankie's, though. A mining community with the pit upon which their livelihood depended at its very heart. They managed to set up a Sports and Social Club, funding it by regular donations of one penny a week. A wooden building, it was given the nickname of the 'twisted coupler', referring to the way in which two underground tubs were linked together. It was another decade or two, however, before pithead baths and canteen facilities arrived on the scene. Working conditions were difficult but this colliery prided itself on maintaining an excellent safety record.

Except for just once!

It was a perfectly ordinary Thursday morning, 3rd September 1931. People had set off for their work; night workers had left theirs and returned to their homes. Children played, knowing their long holiday was almost ended. The world was reasonably peaceful, at least as much as the world ever is. It was peaceful at Nuneaton at all events. That is until around ten o'clock, when the earth shook with the violence of an enormous explosion. People were halted in their tracks. From the direction of the sound, it must have been at the colliery and those above ground moved swiftly to seek out the cause.

It was found to have happened in stall no 11, sited at the northernmost end of the colliery, a mile and a half from the main shaft and on rising ground, a steep hill, in fact.

The colliery rescue team got on to the job with commendable speed and other teams turned up from collieries nearby, to wait until their help was needed. To reach the ill-fated stall no 11 was very difficult indeed; pieces of coal kept falling, and the long trek and gradient hampered the rescuers. Eleven men had been working in this stall. Four were already dead, and the remaining seven had ghastly injuries. To get these men out of the smoke and debris, back along the long trail and then up to the surface, was no mean feat and took several hours, always with the distinct possibility of another explosion, more gas, another fall.

The local newspaper, the *Midland Daily Telegraph*, early on the scene, described the injuries as fearful. The flesh of the dead men had almost been seared off and their hair burned. The injured were all in a serious condition and four of them were to die in the ensuing weeks, making a total of eight fatalities. One of the sad deaths was that of a young miner, aged 24, who had been transferred to that ill-omened stall just two days earlier and who, five weeks previously, had been a happy bridegroom. His young wife, being comforted by a neighbour, said she had felt a premonition of disaster. Her husband had brought her a cup of tea before setting off to his work, and she had begged him not to go. This 'uncanny feeling' stayed with her after he left the house; if only he had listened to her.

The first of the bodies to be brought to the surface was that of a man called Miles. They said that when the thick pall of smoke had abated, Miles was clearly seen, sitting on the ground, leaning against a prop with his food ('snap') tin on the floor beside him and his water bottle alongside. They could not quite understand why he simply sat there, did not respond when they called out. . . When they got near to him, they realised he was dead.

The *Midland Daily Telegraph* diligently sought out the survivors and many column inches were devoted to their harrowing stories. There was nothing but praise for the rescue team. Other teams had been standing by but space was limited down below in stall no 11 and, in the main, Newdigate men had rescued Newdigate men.

There were quite a few mysteries about this explosion, and they have still not been solved. Firstly, there was nothing whatsoever to indicate the possible presence of gas; there was no damage to timbering; miners working in the vicinity, but not actually *in* stall no 11, had no idea things were amiss, yet others far away did hear the explosion. There seems to have been considerable doubt as to what equipment was being used in this stall at the time. But it was known that the electric conveyor was operated continuously, and it was possible a spark from this conveyor might, just might, have ignited gas. Investigations went on for a long time, but no real verdict was ever reached.

A relief fund was started. The miners themselves organised this, and the stallmen of Newdigate Colliery started it off with a Lodge donation of £20, also making it clear that they intended to be the body responsible for this fund. They each agreed to give one shilling and to ask all other miners, throughout the entire colliery, to donate sixpence apiece. Money was sent from other sources, and the *Midland Daily Telegraph* donated 15 guineas.

And somebody, it is not known exactly who, wrote a poem!

This was, apparently, a tradition among miners in the old days after pit accidents. Before, of course, the by now somewhat doubtful advantages of nationalisation. A person, or perhaps more than one person, would produce a poem. This was then printed – a bit like the broadsheets of Victorian times – and sold on the streets for a few coppers. In the case of the Newdigate poem, it was threepence. All the proceeds went to the fund to help the dependants of those miners who had lost their lives, leaving wives and children without a breadwinner.

The poems, as you may well imagine, read more like doggerel than verse, but they were made by men more used to handling picks than pens and there is no doubt that they were labours of heartfelt sympathy:

> *3rd September 1931*
> *In Aid of Dependants of*
> *Newdigate Colliery Disaster.*

At this Colliery in Nuneaton
This disaster occurred one day
And eight of our brave working men
Lost their lives in an unfortunate way.

They left their homes that morning
To go down into the depths of hell
To earn their daily living, and bread
For the ones they loved so well.

These men had started working
And perhaps were humming a song
They were all doing their duty
Unaware of what was coming along.

When suddenly an explosion took place
Leaving a deadly gas there
And these brave men were left to face
That which no human soul could bear.

> Rescuers tried their utmost
> And worked themselves out of breath
> But the dark angel had flown through this pit
> Leaving its toll of death.
>
> Men, Women and Children stood at the Pithead,
> Waiting for news from below
> When it was brought many tears were shed
> And many homes wrecked we know.
>
> Heartbroken Wives, Mothers and Children
> Are left in this world today
> May God above protect them
> And help them on their way.

And the final verse reads:

> Farewell dear friends our life is past
> May you and We unite at last
> Mourn not for us nor sorrow make
> But love our children for our sake.

Rest in Peace

Eventually, as in the normal way of things, the dead were buried with respect and reverence, their dependants helped as much as possible, the injured nursed back to health; the safety men had finished their work and come up out of the pit, and once more the miners went down into it and resumed their daily working.

Time moved on, the wounds left by this disaster began to heal over, and strange things began to happen at the north end of pit, where the explosion had taken place. The north end was the loneliest place in the whole of the collier as it was usual for men positioned at that end to work in small numbers, even sometimes on their own. It was an eerie place, and even confirmed sceptics would get a bit fanciful in such a situation.

But it wasn't all fancy. Sometimes there was a kind of mist at this north end; shadows; a sudden appearing and fading away; a feeling of cold; an uncanny sensation. One or two miners mentioned having seen a shadowy figure, but they spoke of it in a sort of shamefaced way, half apologetic. More often than not, those reporting seeing 'something odd' would be the butt of the odd joke, be laughed at, and would eventually just keep quiet about it.

Then, one night, in the middle of the night shift, there was alarm and panic at the north end. A miner, new to the colliery, had been discovered close to the once fated stall no 11, in a state of total collapse. The man was very obviously ill, in a bad state and so shocked he was unable to utter a single word. Whatever it was that had caused him such terror must have been horrific, for in his desperate efforts to escape from it the man had run, full pelt, as fast as he could for half a mile up the gradient, the notorious 1-in-5 that had caused such problems way back in 1931. And then, wordlessly, he had crumpled to the ground. He was rushed immediately to hospital.

A couple of days later, when he had recovered, he told them what he had seen. He had paused in his work, mopped his forehead and then noticed a mist, advancing and receding. As it cleared a little he saw a man, a miner, sitting with his back against a prop, his snap tin on the floor beside him. He was wearing a cap, a tweed cap of an old fashioned style and cut, he had a lamp of the kind miners had used many years previously and his trousers were tied beneath his knees with strings – 'yawped' is the term used for this in Warwickshire; many trades as well as miners would tie strings below the knee.

The watching miner, mopping away his sweat and coal dust, called out to the man; just a simple greeting. The man rose to his feet, looked at the miner with piercing eyes, turned around, and vanished. Just vanished, and the quite heavy mist just melted away.

This had frightened the solitary miner half to death. But later, when the story was told around Arbury, many others admitted to seeing this ghost at the northern end of the pit. He had apparently become a bit of a joke between the regulars up there, and had gained the nickname of 'Old Cloth Cap' because that is what he always wore.

It seems he was usually seen sitting down in the same place, or just walking up and down at the north end. Because he was obviously no threat, they had all just got used to him, and they took no notice. They had arrived at the conclusion, rightly or wrongly, that he was the ghost of one of the dead from the 1931 explosion. 'He harms nobody, so let him be . . .' was the general opinion.

We do not know who Old Cloth Cap was. Nor do we know what has happened to him now, for in 1982 the Newdigate Colliery, Frankie's, closed down. Coal production ceased on 5th February 1982. Thus ended an era; an epoch. This was the first Warwickshire colliery to produce seven thousand tons of coal in one week from a single coalface. In June 1966, that was!

In its 84 years of vigorous life, the colliery provided work for more than four generations of Bedworth menfolk, and those from elsewhere too. They called it 'a family pit', 'a good little pit' and they mourned its passing. The community drank a toast to a dying way of life, and the last, the very last, lump of coal was polished and beautifully mounted to be put on display in the Social Club lounge.

Perhaps, with all this, Old Cloth Cap is now put to rest too.

THE SPERNALL SHOOTIST

Blood is thicker than water, so they say. But they are wrong, for it is rarely if ever true. Sharing the same blood and the same genes does not glue any family together unless its members want it to do so. And even then it is not necessarily either blood or genes, but most likely the genuine love and respect which each member has for others of his family. James Crowley could tell you all about this if you were to ask him. Only you cannot for he isn't here any more. They hanged him!

The word for 'if' is probably the most threadbare in any language, so frequently is it used. But if James Crowley's father, William Crowley, had been just a little more sensible; had been just a little bit more of a caring parent, had died one year earlier instead of one year later, the tragic events of that fearful day in 1842 need never have happened. But they did. William was a foolish and insensitive man, having favourites among his many offspring, then chopping and changing, transferring his affections from one to another, playing each off against the others. Thus he achieved a miserable and most unhappy household.

William Crowley was a farmer in a well-to-do way of business, at Spernall, not far from Alcester. Spernall was very small and somewhat insignificant, consisting merely of a farm or two, a few rather pleasant cottages, a fine rectory and once upon a time Henry Teonge, the notable diarist, whose work gives a wonderful picture of life in the navy at that time, was rector here. As ever in such a small hamlet, everybody knew everybody, and the Crowley family were well known to their neighbours and much gossiped about.

William had been twice married, and by each wife had produced a large brood. James Crowley was a child of the second marriage, and from an early age he did not see eye to eye with his father at all. Why this should be so has never been made clear. William seems to have been a perverse, obtuse and obstinate man, resentful of many things, including his own family. He didn't really get on with any of his children, and he treated them shamefully. James, however, was by all accounts a bit brighter than the others and perhaps had a bit more spirit, and as a consequence was the permanent object of parental ire and anger. At one stage, so distressed and upset was he by treatment meted out to him that he had fly-sheets printed and distributed locally in order to let his friends and neighbours know about what he called the brutality and maltreatment to which he was subject.

This was the last straw for father William and, without more ado, James was thrown out of the family home. He went to live in a hovel-like cottage, still on his father's farmland. It was derelict and not especially comfortable or warm, but James considered the latest row would eventually blow over and he would be allowed to return home.

William then declared to all and sundry – indeed to anyone who would listen – that he had become afraid of James, fearful of what the boy might do. He considered himself in danger, and accordingly he had one of his own farm labourers sworn in as a special constable. In the days of which we speak, men could be sworn in as 'specials' to cover almost any contingency, real or imagined, that might arise, and they could not refuse. Refusals resulted in harsh penalties. So, William Tilsley, farmhand, living in a tied cottage on the farm of his employer, had to agree, whether he wanted to or not, and was accordingly appointed, primarily to protect William Crowley against whatever his son James might or might not do. And Tilsley had to look pleased about it!

Christmas morning, 1842. A time when hearts are supposed to soften and families are wont to gather together, knee-deep in peace and goodwill! James Crowley, in his hovel, rose and dressed in his everyday working clothes. He found that he had little food in the house and decided to ride to his father's farm, thinking he might join the family for Christmas Day breakfast. He might (he did not say) have considered this to be a tentative olive branch, but if he did, it did not work. William met him at the door of the farmhouse and, taking up the stance of an archetypal Victorian patriarch, told James, 'Go, and never darken my door again. . .' James did indeed go, watched by his mother and father; he had no choice but his head and his heart were full of bitterness.

Back in his own cottage, James washed, shaved and dressed in his best Sunday clothes; a handsome suit, for James Crowley was not yet 30 and liked good cloth and cut. He had accepted an invitation to eat Christmas dinner with the Garner family who lived but a short ride away. James was paying his addressses to one of the daughters, a Miss M.E. Garner, a lady whom he frequently declared he loved dearly. It seems his advances were looked upon with favour by the Garner family.

He was ready, his horse saddled and waiting, when, turning over the events of the morning in his mind, he suddenly decided to ride once more to his father's house and take issue with his hard-hearted parent. Later he explained he wanted to 'claim his natural right of inheritance, and the privilege of walking peaceably into his family home'. He took with him his gun, for the sole purpose, he explained, of intimidation in case he was threatened.

He found the door locked against him, but saw his mother and father in the front kitchen. He waved the gun to show them, to prove he was serious in his desire to enter his father's house. This did not cause them to unlock the door, and so James walked round to the back entrance of the farmhouse and, as he neared it, he saw Special Constable Tilsley and another couple of farm labourers coming towards him at a run, having been ordered to do so by William Crowley.

In that instant, with no word spoken on either side, James raised the gun. He said he had intended to fire above their heads, but all was hurry and confusion, and before he knew it the gun went off. Tilsley fell to the ground, shot in the head. His companions hurried towards him, but Tilsley was beyond their aid. He had died instantly.

James Crowley was to swear time and again he had no

intention of killing Tilsley, entertained no malice towards the man, although he did point out that Tilsley was authorised to drag him out of the house had he ever been able to gain entrance and was also empowered to beat him about the head with a wooden bludgeon. In addition James pointed out – with truth – that had he wished to shoot his father, he could have easily done so more or less at any time.

After seeing Tilsley fall, James made off at a run, heading towards the stable where he had earlier tethered his horse and taking the gun with him. At that stage, no one tried to stop him; they were engaged in trying to help the unfortunate special constable. Other labourers came hurrying, drawn thither by the noise and shouting. A Dr Morris of Studley was sent for, and upon arrival he pronounced Tilsley dead from a bullet in the head.

Everyone was talking at once, all telling a different tale, and at the very centre of the to-do Tilsley lay dead upon the ground, and James Crowley got clean away. He was not seen again for a very long time. No pursuit was organised, no serious searching was carried out, and it was later, much later, hinted that this was because James Crowley's brother, Joseph, was a special constable also and had deliberately allowed James to escape arrest. There could have been two reasons for this. Maybe he preferred brother James out of the way, rather than disgracing the family name by standing trial in a court of law; or was it a mild and touching burst of brotherly affection? If so, it was certainly the only indication of any affection ever between any members of that ill-fated family.

Then it was learned that James had fled to America.

As always, this 'nine days wonder' ceased to be a wonder any more; rumours died, and almost two years passed rapidly by. Then on 14th December 1844, James Crowley was sitting quietly having a drink in the Castle and Falcon inn in Chester. Suddenly the door was flung wide and in burst two constables, named Taylor and Lee. They pushed towards James shouting 'Consider yourself our prisoner' and without more ado clapped handcuffs upon him. He did not seem surprised when they told him they were arresting him for murder.

It seems he had for some time been living in Chester under an assumed name. Upon his return from America, he had written first to his father on 2nd October 1844, begging for help, describing himself as heartily sorry and signing himself as 'Your truly affectionate, penitent and most miserable son'. Nothing much seems to have come from this letter, and on 16th November 1844 he wrote in the same vein to his mother, asking for her help and quoting the Bible and Rachel who 'weeps for her children and will not be comforted because they are not. . .'

But nothing came of this letter either. Except, of course, the two eager constables, Taylor and Lee. Who it was that 'grassed' upon James Crowley, we do not know. Perhaps his parents or others of the family, who would be aware his whereabouts from the two letters. Certainly Taylor and Lee had no difficulty in finding him.

James Crowley later complained of the way the constables treated him when they arrested him. He declared that they had twisted his arms, and had put a twitch, a sort of tourniquet, upon one arm, turning it and turning it until the string was so tight that his hand turned black. They had then proceeded to empty his pockets, removing some thirty-five sovereigns which they had deliberately miscounted in order to keep some for themselves. 'They acted gleefully in consideration of a reward,' he said.

He had not received his money back, and it was a local magistrate who had ordered the twitch to be removed from his arm. Crowley had offered no resistance on his arrest, and there had been no reason at all for this restraint to be used; it had caused him much pain. They had started out from Chester and had stayed overnight in Birmingham, at an inn, where there had been more 'goings-on' and jokes in relation to the sovereigns taken from Crowley's pocket. These had been counted into piles before the landlady of the inn, and the two constables had told her she must be prepared to be a witness to the number of the sovereigns, and to their honesty.

James Crowley was brought to trial at Warwick Assizes on 4th April 1845. In the dock James, dressed in a handsome suit of black, bowed respectfully to the judge, Mr Justice Maule, and he

Warwick gaol where James Crowley was hanged. (Warwickshire Record Office – Ref PH 143/65a)

pleaded 'Not Guilty'. The press said he looked pale of countenace, dejected and confounded.

However, despite the truly excellent work of his defence attorney, Crowley was found guilty. The jury told the crowded courtroom they had brought in this verdict with the utmost reluctance.

The defence – the only possible defence really – was that of insanity. William Crowley, James's father, had died of natural causes the previous year, and Joseph Crowley, brother to James, was closely questioned about the family.

Joseph had inherited two farms from his father. William had seven children by his first wife and five by his second. The insanity of William's children by his first wife was beyond doubt. Five of them were in institutions, some having attempted suicide – sometimes more than once. William Crowley's conduct through-out almost the whole of his life had been strange, verging upon madness. This was shown especially in his dealings with his children, all except Joseph who seems to have been a favourite, lasting longer in favour than any of the others.

William Crowley and his second wife, the mother of James, were first cousins and several of that lady's nieces, her own blood relations, were already in institutions for the insane when they married. Therefore, the prisoner, James Crowley, hadn't stood much of a chance, having had the misfortune to inherit insanity from both mother and father.

James bore all of this with dignity and composure. He did not like the defence of insanity, but had been persuaded it was the only way to defend him. Like most people who are unbalanced he was convinced he was the sanest person on the face of the earth. But he had shot Tilsley. In using the plea of insanity to the jury, Crowley's excellent and kind attorney had even pointed out that James had been safe enough in America but had chosen to return and suffer himself to be arrested. 'Is this the action of a sane man?' he asked.

James was found guilty and sentenced to be hanged, with the full panoply of the law. His life was to end at the age of a mere 31 years.

It was later reported that at the time of the trial there were many witnesses within the court who had come prepared to testify to the insanity of James Crowley, immediately prior to and during his offence! But, because of some legal technicality, they were not examined.

However, they were gathered up and their testimonies in the form of affidavits, ten in number, written out. Crowley's attorney wrote to the Home Secretary, then Sir James Graham, setting out the circumstances, enclosing the affidavits and pleading for clemency.

Others wrote in the same vein. The entire jury contacted him, saying that they had found Crowley guilty but had forgotten to add their pleas for mercy.

But none of it did a bit of good. Sir James said he felt he would not be warranted in 'interfering'.

James Crowley behaved impeccably. He wrote personal letters of thanks to all those who had laboured on his behalf. He wrote to his beloved Miss Garner who had visited him in prison. He wrote letters for publication in the press thanking readers for the many expressions of support and for their prayers.

On 18th April 1845, James Crowley was hanged, and his very last words in this world were: 'I did not intend to shoot that man (Tilsley) so help me God. . .'

William Tilsley, just a humble farm labourer of those days, had been forced into becoming a special constable. He made an honest attempt to do his duty. To him falls the doubtful distinction of being the very first special constable to be killed in the course of his duty in Warwickshire.

He was shot dead by James Crowley, who was then hanged by the neck until he was dead! The question is – if Crowley was indeed insane, and there is much evidence of this – should he have been hanged at all?

* * * *

POSTCRIPT: Sometime in the early 1930s, an old lady living in the vicinity of Henley-in-Arden achieved her century. No mean feat in those days. She was interviewed by a reporter, who asked her for her recollections. 'When I was a little maid', she said, 'I worked at the White Swan Hotel in Henley-in-Arden High Street. One day I was told to take a sup of ale to the man sitting on his horse outside in front of the hotel. I did as I was bidden. The man drank down the ale, thanked me, and handed back the jug. So nice, he was,' she said. 'Such a nice face and kind eyes. Then two constables came out of the hotel, and they all rode off.' Later, she had asked who the man was, and learned he was James Crowley, the murderer. 'I could not believe he was a murderer,' she said. 'He looked so kind. . .'

THE MAN WHO SAVED HITLER

When the local newspaper, the *Leamington Courier*, carried the headline 'At War with Germany. England Forced to Fight' the entire town of Leamington Spa was enveloped in a patriotic fervour that was almost tangible. The *Courier* exhorted its readers and they responded with perhaps lamentable vigour! Ladies trotted around handing out white feathers without determining whether or not these were justified; people told each other on no account to buy goods made in Germany; and anyone who appeared to have German connections, no matter how tenuous, was serenely snubbed. One innocent and bewildered shopkeeper wrote to the newspaper pointing out he had bought items made in Germany *before* the country was at war, and how could he have known the two countries were getting ready to fight each other? Now with a stock of German goods he was likely to end up bankrupt, and it wasn't his fault! The *Courier* printed a poem from a local lad at the front:

> Here's to the Leamington volunteeers
> That go and enlist today
> There's plenty joining Kitcheners
> To help us in the fray
> So buck up dear old Leamington
> If you want to see the fun
> For you think the war is over
> When it's only just begun.

This was quite early in the proceedings, in October 1914, and it was not long before the lads from Leamington, and indeed the lads from elsewhere and anywhere, realised only too bitterly and too well that it was far from fun, and it certainly would not be, as was often suggested, 'over by Christmas'.

One young man, employed as assistant engineer at the town's leading and most prestigious hotel, the Regent, needed none of this urging. He had already joined the Army prior to the official declaration of war, and he was to become the most decorated private soldier of the First World War, bringing much honour to Leamington Spa, the town of his birth.

Later, much later, when writing of his exploits, the *Daily Telegraph* referred to Private Henry Tandey, VC, DCM, MM, as 'A Hero of the old Berserk Type', as indeed well they might, for his daring, his vast courage and his obstinate refusal to quit were astonishing.

Henry Tandey, known as 'Harry' or sometimes 'Napper' (although no one seems to know the reason for this latter name), was born in Leamington Spa in 1891, eldest son of a military, though humble, family. His parents lived in Livery Street in the town, and his grandfather, James Tandey, lived in Leicester Street. James Tandey was a very reputable and well respected marble mason who had carried out work for the notable and fashionable George Gilbert Scott, and was perhaps the longest established such tradesman in the town at the time, towards the end of the century.

Tandey's father served in the 16th Lancers in the South African Wars and was called up as a reservist in the Great War. Henry's brothers, James and Samuel, were also serving, Samuel being wounded at the Battle of Jutland. So, the Tandey menfolk served their country well.

Henry Tandey was in the Green Howards and later attached to the 5th Bn The Duke of Wellington's West Riding Regiment. It was at Marcoing in France that he won the DCM, for 'determined bravery and initiative', in a battle lasting from 25th August to 2nd September 1918. Tandey was in charge of a reserve bombing party in an attack on a system of trenches. Finding the parties in front

Private Henry Tandey, VC, DCM, MM.

temporarily held up, he grabbed a couple of volunteers from his own party, worked his way across the open ground and rushed the enemy post, killing several Germans and taking twenty prisoners.

Only ten days later, again at Marcoing, on 12th September, the MM was conferred upon Tandey for 'great heroism and devotion to duty'. He went out under heavy shell fire, found a wounded comrade and carried him back. Immediately, he went out again and rescued three more men. Then during a bombing attack on the Hindenburg line on the following day, he volunteered to be the leading bomber, and led the party into the open. He made himself responsible for holding the bombing block in the trench, and while he was doing this, the post was attacked by the enemy in strength. The German officer faced Tandey and shot him at almost point blank range, and . . . missed! Tandey, quite regardless of danger, led his party against the enemy and drove them off in total confusion. Tandey's conduct was described as 'of the highest order of gallantry and determined leadership beyond all praise'.

Only about two weeks after this, on 28th September and again at Marcoing, Henry Tandey won the Victoria Cross 'for the most conspicuous bravery during the capture of the village and crossings'. Tandey's platoon was held up by gunfire. He crawled forward, located the machine gun and knocked it out. He then reached the crossings and restored a plank bridge under a hail of bullets so that the first crossing could be made at this vital spot. During the same evening, he and eight comrades were totally surrounded and completely outnumbered. Their position was hopeless. But Henry Tandey did not know the word 'hopeless' and he led a bayonet charge through the lot of them, fighting so fiercely that thirty-seven of the enemy were driven into the hands of the remainder of his own Company. He was wounded, but refused to leave until the fight was won.

Tandey was mentioned five times in despatches; he was seriously wounded three times and yet miraculously survived. Throughout his entire army service, he persistently refused promotion saying, simply, that he didn't want it and wished to remain a private.

Private Tandey recovered from his wounds and was at

Buckingham Palace on 19th December 1919 to receive the Victoria Cross from his King.

On this day, the *Daily Mirror* burst into verse and decided to toast Tandey thus:

> Good luck to Tandey and good health
> Upon the field his pluck was tested
> If such men are the Nation's wealth
> Tis good to see them well invested.

And the *Telegraph* gave its opinion that the 'man in the street', that ubiquitous character we hear so much about, would consider Tandey's courage to have earned him the Victoria Cross three times over!

Tandey was honoured by being made a Freeman of Leamington Spa, with the parade, the casket and all the proper and appropriate ceremony. He was chosen to be one of fifty VCs to line the aisles of Westminster Abbey for the burial of the Unknown Soldier. He remained in the Army until 1926. But that is not the whole story. There is an ironic twist to this tale, for Henry Tandey, albeit completely unwittingly, changed the course of history on 28th September 1918, the day on which his courage won him Britain's highest honour, the VC.

Henry Tandey, quiet 'Napper' Tandey, was an honourable man. More – he was a man *of* honour. To him the path of duty was perfectly clear, and he always did what he considered to be the right thing.

On 28th September 1918, the battle raged furiously. Tandey and his comrades fought beneath a hail of bullets; fought amid machine gun fire; fought the enemy, the Germans, hand-to-hand; fought to the sound of wounded men screaming; fought thinking it unlikely they would see the end of that day and live. Tandey in the middle of it all was shouting, moving forward, and then quite suddenly he saw in front of him an injured German, a corporal, fall to the ground. Tandey had the man at his mercy, but although he paused, he could not bring himself to shoot someone who was helpless, even one of the enemy. So he moved on, leaving the

Tandey carrying a wounded soldier as depicted in Mantania's painting, a print of which was requested by Hitler.

wounded corporal to struggle back to his own lines for help.

The fighting went on, battles went on, the mud went on – and the war continued until its bitter end. The fate of this lone German soldier was long forgotten. Except by that very soldier himself, who never forgot. For the name of that fallen corporal was Adolf Hitler!

Adolf Hitler came to power in 1933. He had often wondered about the identity of the British soldier who had spared his life. He set his staff to search through British Army records, with special attention to the action at Marcoing, and they discovered that the private soldier who had led the attack against Hitler's platoon was Henry Tandey.

We then come to the Italian war artist, Fortunio Mantania. He was at the front much of the time, sketching many scenes and sending them to various newspapers. He had sketched Tandey and later turned the drawing into a painting showing Tandey carrying a wounded comrade to safety at the Menin crossroads action in October 1914, four years before the Marcoing action.

Hitler was told of this painting, which hung in the officers' mess at the Regimental Depot of the Green Howards in Yorkshire. Hitler had himself been involved in the Menin action, and instructed a certain Dr Schwend to write requesting a copy of this picture. The Green Howards obliged; Hitler received a copy and, seeing Tandey, declared this was the man who had spared his life. The Fuhrer hung the painting on the wall of his mountain retreat at Berchtesgaden, and a Capt Weidmann wrote to the officers of the Green Howards to tell them how pleased the Fuhrer was with their 'gift of friendship'. It is said that Hitler was much moved by the painting.

Meanwhile Tandey got on with his life, and had not the slightest idea of any of this.

In 1938 our Prime Minister, Neville Chamberlain, visited Hitler in a last ditch and desperate attempt at 'peace in our time'. We all know now that it was a vain hope, but it was worth a try. Hitler, a good host, showed Chamberlain around his Berchtesgaden retreat and pointed out to him the Menin picture. 'That', declared the Fuhrer with conviction, 'is the man who spared my life. That man came so near to killing me I thought I would never see Germany ever again.'

Chamberlain knew nothing of this story, but he listened politely and promised Hitler that upon his return to England he would locate Tandey and pass on to him the Fuhrer's thanks and good wishes.

Tandey was, by this time, living in Coventry and working at the Standard Motor Company. You may imagine his total astonishment when he received a 'phone call from the Prime Minister passing on the Fuhrer's greetings. Tandey, when questioned by the press, said, 'They say I've met Adolf Hitler. Maybe they're right, but I can't remember him.' He said he recalled the incident with the wounded German corporal, but he never looked at his face. Over and over again, when this story was told, Tandey said with complete honesty that he just did not know! However, members of this family said that when he saw photographs of Hitler in the newspapers from time to time, and prior to Chamberlain's telephone call, he had remarked there was 'something a bit familiar' about the man.

Later, much later, and especially after the bombing of Coventry in November 1940, Tandey was more adamant. 'When I see all the women and children Hitler has killed and wounded, I'm sorry to God I let him go. . .'

During the 1939-45 conflict, Private Henry Tandey became Sergeant Tandey, a recruiting sergeant. He attended with pride all reunions of VCs and other ceremonies held in London from 1920 until 1968, and he was present at a very special reunion at Strenshall Camp, Yorkshire, in September 1968. This, basically, was to mark the 50th anniversary of the end of the First World War and was also a kind of tribute to Henry Tandey, who had won all his well deserved honours in the month of September.

Some four hundred old comrades of the Green Howards turned up to meet each other, and one hundred of them were from the 1914-18 conflict. Trenches were dug on waste land, 'Blighty' signs were put up and the men were treated to tin hats, beer, sausages and mouth organ music. A whale of time was had by all.

Henry Tandey died at his home in Coundon, Coventry on 20th

December 1977, aged 86. His body was cremated, and his ashes taken to France and scattered at Marcoing where, as a young soldier, he had served so bravely and so well.

His widow Annie, his second wife, sold Tandey's medals at Sotheby's in 1980, and they were brought by a private collector for the record sum of £27,000. This was at least £10,000 more than the previous price paid for such a group of medals.

Tandey's home town of Leamington Spa desperately wanted these medals, and the Mayor, at that time Mr Norman Parker, raised a great deal of money towards their purchase from a consortium that included Warwick District Council, the Regent Hotel, Leamington businessmen and the Victoria and Albert Museum. Mr Parker sat for hours at Sotheby's waiting for the medals to come up but, alas, he was outbid. He did ask the purchaser why he had bought the medals, and was told it was to prevent them leaving Britain. They have now been generously given to the Regimental Museum and are thus in safe hands. Mr Parker said it was a great disappointment to him and to the town, but 'we had to draw a line under it'.

Leamington Spa might not have the medals, but they can still take pride in the bravery of Henry Tandey, the most decorated private soldier of the First World War. But the mystery remains. Did Tandey save Hitler's life? Military archivists say the incident happened. And others remember that Tandey was a quiet and modest man; rarely talked of his exploits; refused promotion; refused to let the media turn him into a 'star'. So would such a man have allowed such a story to be told unless it were ture? Now supposing he had not let the corporal live, what course do you think history would have taken?

LEAMINGTON AND THE CZECH PATRIOTS

Leamington Spa, founded as they used to tell you upon a puddle of water, was one of our most gracious towns, and still retains much charm. But, for just a brief moment, consider how truly delightful it must have been in the halcyon days immediately prior to 1939 before the skies darkened above all our towns. There were wide tree-lined streets; green open spaces; gentle music by a string quartet in the famous Pump Rooms where you might choose to take tea; shops where assistants hurried to set a chair for their customers so that purchases might be discussed at ease; prestigious hotels with uniformed staff, establishments that had once played host to the cream of society arriving for the season and to take the waters. Lawn tennis was invented at one such hotel, whilst at the other end of the town were courts where 'real tennis' – the game of kings – was greatly enjoyed.

It was not a crowded town. It was quiet, polite, relaxed and above all sure of itself and its place in the scheme of things. This is where many retired service people came to live, in flats, or perhaps suites in hotels, and inevitably they indulged in that wonderful cure-all, taking the waters.

The war came and everything was changed for everybody, the length and breadth of our country. Nothing was ever to be the same again. Leamington Spa, just a little complacent perhaps, was shaken to the core when it was invaded! Yes, invaded by thousands of foreign troops. But . . . drawing a collective deep breath, the townspeople rose wonderfully to the occasion and, with great warmth, took the invaders to their hearts. Later, much,

much later, they were to learn of the most daring and terrifying secret plot hatched within their town, and carried out successfully by seven of their guests, all of whom lost their lives in so doing. The town has not forgotten, nor ever will, and upon occasion these men are referred to as 'our Magnificent Seven'.

The Czech army, or what remained of it, came to Leamington in September 1940. The three thousand soldiers had managed to escape from their own land when Hitler sent his troops into Czechoslovakia; they got to France, helped both the French and the British, and then managed (some of them) to escape yet again at the time of Dunkirk. They landed, eventually, in Britain, demoralised, dispirited and with much of their equipment and uniforms lost, and thus came to Leamington to regroup and get themselves properly organised. They came to fight for their homeland, no holds barred.

Accommodation was found for them in houses in and around the town, the main one being a large property in Newbold Terrace, and it was here that plans of great significance were formulated.

Their President, Edouard Benes, in exile in London, was desperate for some action, a coup of some kind to prove to the Allies that the Czechs could and would fight and damage the German war machine. Attempts had been made, and had failed, to guide Allied bombers to the Skoda arms factory outside Prague, and efforts to sabotage trains carrying munitions hadn't been successful either.

So he had another plan, code-named Operation Anthropoid, and he, Benes, personally briefed two of the Czechs stationed in Leamington, Jan Kubis and Josef Gabcik, for this mission which he knew to be utter suicide. They were to strike at the very face of evil; to kill Reinhard Heydrich, head of the Germany Security Service, second only to Himmler himself and the man largely responsible for organising the genocide, the camps, the gas chambers, in short the holocaust, mention of which, even now all these years on, causes most of the world to recoil in horror.

Heydrich was considered the most powerful man in the Third Reich, and it was even whispered he might be a likely successor to

Hitler himself. He was a dangerous man, evil, perverted and one for all to be wary of. And yet he was tall and handsome, with those fair-haired Aryan good looks so much admired in Nazi Germany. In September 1941 Hitler appointed Heydrich 'Protector' of Moravia and Bohemia, and once he got settled in Prague, he began a reign of terror that put the Czech population through hell. Who came up with the plan to assassinate this evil man has never been made very clear. It has been said it was all the idea of the British Secret Service because they had heard Heydrich was about to arrest a very important German traitor who had been supplying information to the British. It has also been said it was in an attempt to stop the extermination of European Jews. And again, others believed the British wanted Heydrich removed because he knew too much about the alleged treasonable activities of the Duke of Windsor in the summer of 1940.

It may just have been that Benes wanted action. The plan was given sanction all round, and sections of the British Secret Service undertook the arduous training of the seven men from Leamington.

It was to be a very complicated operation. Kubis and Gabcik were selected to carry out the actual assassination, and the remaining five were back-up, gathering information, negotiating with the Czech Resistance, relaying messages and all that type of thing.

Kubis and Gabcik had become fast friends; carefully chosen, their personalities and their characters complemented each other perfectly. Their hatred of the Nazis who had driven them from their own homeland was absolute, and in the case of Kubis even more so, if possible, for he bore their mark on his body, where a small row of swastikas has been burned into his flesh.

Things began to go wrong from the very start of the operation. First, the Halifax bomber dropped the men by parachute miles off course, and Gabcik injured his foot painfully when he landed badly. They had to hide and remain hidden, and they had a difficult job trying to convince the Czech Underground that they were NOT spies foisted on them by the Germans in an attempt to discover Resistance secrets. Information was not easy to come by, and they were all too well aware they were endangering the lives of any Czech people who might help them. In order to plan the death of the hated Heydrich, they needed details of his every movement.

How to do it? It was impossible to get near the man at home or at work, and therefore grabbing him by the throat, knifing him, a garrotte, or the combat in which they had been particularly trained were all totally ruled out. Heydrich was heavily guarded both in his private accommodation and in the headquarters which he had set up in some style at Hradcany Castle. However, he did commute some fifteen miles between home and work, arrogantly insisting on travelling without escort in an open top Mercedes. He considered he had cowed the Czech people enough so they'd never dare to attack his person. He was wrong, of course! He was always chauffeur driven and did the journey really fast, 'bat out of hell' style, so a bullet wasn't going to be the answer either.

Sometimes Heydrich travelled to Berlin by special trains, and although the conspirators managed to obtain details of these journeys, more problems presented themselves. They were trained in the use of explosives, but if they blew up the train they would kill others, their own countrymen. It was also possible that Heydrich could escape the wrecked train; he might not even be much injured let alone dead. Too risky and too uncertain.

In the end it was agreed there would have to be an ambush of sorts, and they would have to work it all out with consummate care, for they wouldn't get another chance.

On 27th May 1942, Heydrich was to go to Berlin, and his chauffeur would drive him to Prague airport. It was a fast route and there was one, just one place where an ambush might work. This was a hairpin bend, a corner at Holesovice, where the chauffeur would have no alternative but to slow down a little. Jan Kubis and Josef Gabcik, the two assigned to the deed, hid themselves near the bend, and waited.

The minutes ticked by. The SS Obergruppenfuhrer was late! They were getting a little panicky when they spotted the green Merc approaching at speed, with Heydrich in the front sitting by his chauffeur. The vehicle slowed down for the bend, as anticipated. Gabcik stepped out from the verge, raised his sten gun and fired at almost point blank range. Nothing happened! The gun was faulty and failed to fire. The terrified Gabcik was left, standing there, facing his intended victim, and helpless to do anything about it. If Heydrich had ordered his chauffeur to drive on, to get away, the German leader would have remained alive. But he didn't! He ordered him to stop the car instead, and he got out and faced Gabcik, flourishing his pistol. As he did this, Kubis stepped out from the shadows and lobbed a bomb into the car. Again, misfortune. Kubis misjudged, and instead of landing in the car, it exploded against the rear wheel!

Everything was chaos. Shrapnel, screams, broken glass, and the car was pouring smoke. Kubis, hit by splinters and shrapnel, was blinded by blood. Gabcik seemed paralysed, and was still holding the useless sten. Then the chauffeur, Klein, gave chase as Kubis made a bid for escape, and at the same time, Heydrich with his pistol kept Gabcik pinned behind a telegraph pole. But suddenly, as Gabcik watched unbelieving, Heydrich doubled up, crying out in pain, and keeled over, falling to the ground. Gabcik watched no more, but made off.

The two Czech conspirators managed to get away and later met up. They were desperate, thinking their plan had failed, that Heydrich was unhurt; but it was not so! It transpired that splinters of steel from the exploded car had penetrated Heydrich's back, deep into the spleen and the lumbar region. He was rushed to hospital, but medical attention in the area at that time was a bit sketchy and blood poisoning rapidly set in. The so-called 'Protector' of Bohemia and Moravia died in hospital one week later, and he died as slowly, as horribly and as painfully as he had himself forced so many others to die while he watched their last agonies.

Heydrich's Berlin funeral was very impressive; the streets heavily draped in black and the Berlin Philharmonic playing Wagner. Hitler, greatly moved, referred to him as a 'martyr'.

Meantime, Nazi Intelligence swung into action, and the killing began. With the aid of torture, fear and terror, they indicted a lot of people, and murdered not only those involved, however

The memorial fountain in Jephson Gardens, Leamington Spa. The parachute is shaped in honour of 'the Magnificent Seven'. (Leamington Spa Council)

remotely, but hundreds who had nothing whatever to do with Heydrich's assassination.

The seven Leamington compatriots were still on the run on 10th June, when the Nazis decided unequivocally that the people of Lidice (a village near Prague) had supported and assisted the perpetrators of the assassination, as well as doing other reprehensible and unlawful things like hoarding food and hiding a transmitter.

This was a total fabrication. Nobody in Lidice had anything to do with Heydrich's death. They had never even heard of Jan Kubis or Josef Gabcik. But what cared the Nazis for that? They were intent upon a public revenge and they took it; a most appalling revenge that will never, ever be forgotten.

They descended upon the village. All the men together with

boys over the age of fifteen were taken from their homes, lined up against the wall of a barn and shot, their bodies tipped into a mass grave nearby. All the womenfolk, 195 of them, and 90 children were piled into lorries and sent off to concentration camps, where most of the women died quite soon. Almost all of the children were killed. Eight children were set aside, considered to be suitable for 'Germanisation', and were given to families to be brought up strictly as Germans and not told who they were; not told anything.

But they weren't satisfied even yet. Lorries and bulldozers were brought in to remove all traces of the village. Lidice was razed to the ground, the rubble and all else carted away so that nothing whatsoever remained but a patch of bare earth. This must have pleased the Nazis in some way, for they repeated the process shortly after in a village called Lezaky. By September 1942 more than three thousand Czechs had been murdered to avenge the killing of the 'Protector' Reinhard Heydrich!

The Leamington Seven ultimately sought sanctuary in the crypt of the church of St Cyril and St Methodious in Prague, and on 18th June Nazi troops surrounded it. It was like some ghastly parody of a Western film; a stand-off, with both sides firing. The Czech patriots early realised there was no way out, but they determined to 'take a few with them' and kept on firing until they ran out of ammunition; each one saved his last bullet for himself. At the given signal, standing in line, with a last desperate prayer for their countrymen, the seven men each raised his pistol to his head, and each took his own life.

The Nazis dragged the seven bodies out of the crypt and into the city, where they exhibited the seven severed heads on spikes as a warning to all.

The people of Leamington knew nothing of this until much later. They had enjoyed offering hospitality to the Czechs and the Czechs had done much in return. They had visited hospitals, volunteered for things, organised entertainments, carved wooden toys for children, and by bringing to the people of Leamington a little taste of the culture of a far off country helped to lighten the dull grey wartime days. Many did not return to Czechoslovakia after the war, having met and married local girls. The world famous conductor Vilem Tausky was stationed in Leamington when he met and later married a school teacher from Kenilworth. He also formed a Czech Army Band within the town.

There is a memorial to the brave Czech patriots on the wall of the church where they met their death. But once Leamington got to hear about all the horror, it was decided that another memorial should stand in Leamington, and what better or more appropriate place than on the green lawns of the Jephson Gardens in the centre of the town?

Accordingly a sculpture was commissioned, designed by the School of Art of the mid-Warwickshire College. It is in the form of a fountain to symbolise life, shaped like a parachute and set upon seven pillars coming together in the centre. The citation is thus:

In tribute to all Czechoslovak soldiers, Airmen
and Patriots who fell in World War II. From Royal
Leamington Spa in 1941 volunteers from free Czechoslovak
Forces stationed in the town were parachuted into their
homeland to rid it of the tyrant SS General Heydrich.
Two of them, Jan Kubis and Josef Gabcik, accomplished
their mission in May 1942. They and their companions
laid down their lives for FREEDOM.

Nearby a bronze plaque bears the words 'Lidice Shall Live'.

Each year Czechs come to Leamington from far and wide to visit the memorial and pay their respects to these brave men, 'the Magnificent Seven' indeed.

THE DEATH OF
RANDOLPH TURPIN

'I fought for it, and I'm going to spend it,' declared the young, successful and much admired Randolph Adolphus Turpin, and spend it he certainly did, romping through in excess of £300,000 in his few years in the spotlights. Bearing in mind his spotlight years were in the 1950s, this was an inordinate amount of money for a young man who, for the major part of his life, had been poor, and the Randy Turpin story is one of rags to riches and rapidly back to rags again. In 1966, depressed and deeply in debt, Turpin was found shot through the head, in the attic of his home above a transport cafe in Russell Street, Leamington Spa. He was 38 years old. The Coroner's verdict was that he had taken his own life, and he further ordered that the inquest file should remain closed for 75 years.

The circumstances of the boxer's death remain a mystery, and there are those who knew him well who cannot believe he would die by his own hand, in the rather messy and questionable way he did.

The story of the fighting Turpins begins way back in the 1920s when Lionel Turpin, a negro from British Guiana, came to England after fighting in the trenches of the First World War. Here, he met and married Beatrice Whiteman, daughter of a notable bare knuckle pugilist of the old days. Beatrice and Lionel set up home in a rather miserable basement flat in Willes Road, Leamington and life was far from easy for them. By 1927, Beatrice had given birth to five children: Dick, Joan, Jackie and Kathy, and one little mite who was stillborn. Then on 7th June 1928,

Randolph, the last child, arrived on the scene.

In the 1920s, a white girl married to a black man, and with five mixed race children, had a very hard row to hoe. But Beatrice wasn't the daughter of a fighter for nothing. She could and did hold her own with the best of them, coming out onto the street, fists clenched and arms flailing, ready to deal with any ill-considered remarks or name calling. Later, neighbours said the boys, Dick, Jackie and Randy, got their fighting spirit from their mother.

Although things had not been easy, at least the Turpins were all together and were managing. Then tragedy struck, for Lionel Turpin died, succumbing to the disastrous effects of the gas he had absorbed in the trenches, leaving his young family, with the baby, Randolph, not yet a year old. Beatrice then was cast in the role of sole breadwinner, and she took to scrubbing floors and indeed doing almost anything that would keep her children fed and warm, and the rent paid. But she was losing her battle, and Randolph had still not reached his third birthday when he caught pneumonia. He was very ill and he very nearly died, but he fought for his life – and he won!

Beatrice, however, was not exactly winning at this time and, despite doing all she could, she was forced to split up the family on a temporary basis. Dick went to live with Grandma Whiteman; Joan went to an aunt in Wales; Beatrice's sister, Ethel, took baby Randolph, and Jackie and Kathy stayed with their mother. Beatrice had no intention of being without her children for very long and eventually she managed to rent a flat above Dillons fish and chip shop in Market Place, Warwick, and they all came home.

Then Beatrice married again, a local chap, Ernest Manley, who took on Beatrice and her five children in 1931 and loved them all. In later years, Randolph, who obviously could scarcely remember his own father, would say what a wonderful stepfather Manley had been to them all.

The family upped sticks and moved to Wathen Street, Warwick and it was here that Randolph spent his formative years. When he was five, he went to Westgate Council School and if anything could be said to be his first 'training ground' it was here, for a mere six teachers taught and looked after some three hundred young boys; you had to stick up for yourself if you were of mixed race, and the Turpins did, especialy Randolph. By the time he reached his twelfth birthday, he'd really shown them all, for he could out-punch, out-run, out-swim and out-everything every other lad in the school, and he wasn't finished yet.

He made a best friend here at Westgate School; a lad called Pete Price became his inseparable mate, and remained so. Randy, his brother Jackie and Peter were a threesome, welded together; a gang of three, scarcely ever apart and, naturally enough, forever in some sort of scrape or up to some mischief. Randolph always had a soft spot for animals. He had a pet rabbit for some time and used to take it with him wherever he went. He and Jackie would sneak into nearby fields to ride the horses bareback, and as a result, in later years, Randolph was almost as good a horseman as he was a boxer.

He decided on his future career quite early on, when he was around eight years of age. He and the 'gang' – Pete and Jackie – would stand with noses pressed to the windows of the fish and chip shop, looking at the posters and the photographs of those who had made it in the ring. Pete and Jackie just looked, but Randolph looked intently and said, 'That's what I'm going to do. Be a boxer. . .'

He got a first chance when local businessman George Middleton started a boys' boxing club, and both Jackie and Randolph, armed with some excellent advice from Grandfather Whiteman, joined to become part of the Middleton 'stable'. Middleton kitted them out with fancy dressing gowns, embroidered shorts and the gear, and billed them as Alexander and Moses for some reason.

In 1942 Police Inspector John Gibbs, a true friend to Randolph and who remained his friend to the end of his life, started the Leamington Boys' Club. Randolph and Jackie were among the first members. At the age of 14, Randolph won the ABA Youths' Championship of Great Britain. He was the Junior Champion three times – 1943, 1944, 1945 – and the Senior Champion twice – 1945, 1946.

After leaving school, Randolph worked for Tarvers, a firm of builders, and it was swinging the pick and shovel that kept him in good shape and strengthened his muscles. Randolph turned professional whilst doing his obligatory National Service in the Navy. All three brothers, Dick, Jackie and Randolph were in the fight game, but the youngest was destined to be the star of the Turpins. The brothers promised their mother that they would never on any account fight each other, and this promise was faithfully kept.

Randolph married Mary Stack, a local girl referred to in the press as his 'childhood sweetheart', but the marriage was a disaster and the couple separated. There was a son, though, Young Randolph, adored by his father and all the Turpin family. Randolph and Mary were eventually divorced, but not without pain and acrimony on both sides.

Randolph was all too frequently in 'women trouble'. Stories abound, and perhaps not all of them are true. He was young, good looking; he was a star, much admired in the press; and he was making a lot of money. So . . . women flocked to him and he enjoyed the flattery and adulation.

After the Navy, Randolph was back in Warwick and in training. He was determined and it was not long before he obtained his first important professional bout. In October 1950 he won the British middleweight title by knocking out Albert Finch in the 5th round. This seemed appropriate at that time, for brother Dick had lost this title to Albert Finch only the year before, and now here it was, back with the Turpins. Randolph then went on to become European middleweight champion, taking this title from Lucien Van Dam of Holland.

And then came the big one; the one he had been aiming for. The World middleweight title was his after he beat Sugar Ray Robinson, on points, at Earls Court in July 1951.

He was World Champ; he was a hero; he was the 'Leamington Licker' who had proved he could 'lick' anybody. Never had quiet Leaming Spa been in such a ferment. He was given a hero's welcome; he rode up the Parade seated between the Mayor of Leamington and the Mayor of Warwick, who at this time

Randolph Turpin – Middleweight Champion of the World. (Leamington Spa Courier)

happened to be the Earl of Warwick.

There was a civic dinner in his honour and the streets were thronged. The cheering rose to a crescendo and when he appeared on the balcony of the Town Hall, leading his mother Beatrice, now rather frail, by the hand and was seen to give her a hug, there wasn't a dry eye anywhere! Dancing went on in the streets until the early hours.

This was his big moment, his finest hour, and it was never to be like this again. Two months later he lost the title in a return bout with Sugar Ray Robinson, when the referee stopped the fight in the 10th round.

It was while he was in New York for this that he encounted 24 year old Adele Daniels, who later sued him for assault, calling him vicious and cruel. This case dragged on and was eventually settled out of court. Meantime, a policeman in Lancashire obtained a divorce and cited Randolph Turpin as his wife's lover.

He bought a 29 bed hotel in Llandudno with his fight money, and that rapidly failed. He bought suits. At one count he had more than 30. He bought cars. But in his favour, he was generous to his family, and gave them many things.

Then he met 26 year old Gwen Price, daughter of a Welsh farmer. The press, on to anything about Randolph, hounded them a little and they married in November 1952 amid speculation and rather unnecessary secrecy. Randolph did not even tell his mother, and she informed the press that her new daughter-in-law 'would not be welcome in my house'.

Randolph spent much of his time on the Welsh farm, helping with hay, the animals and indeed anything that required doing. All his life he was to have a strong affection for Wales and when, after a year, his daughter Gwyneth was born he bought a house there.

Though he had lost his World title, he was still British and European middleweight champion, and in June 1952 he beat Don Cockell and won the British and Empire light-heavyweight title. At the end of 1952, he won his fifth title, Empire middleweight, when he took this from the holder George Angelo.

Turpin's manager, George Middleton, was uneasy about Randolph living in Wales. He wanted him under his eye; wanted to supervise his training very closely. There had been problems with this in the past. Randolph was persuaded, so he and Gwen returned to Leamington and bought an eight-roomed house in St Mary's Road.

In 1952, the World middleweight title was vacant because Sugar Ray had not obeyed the rules; he had not defended his title every six months. Randolph planned a go at this title. He defeated Humez of France with a points win in an elimination bout. Then he met the United States Champ, Carl 'Bobo' Olsen, in New York in October 1953, but lost on points. The press said he looked tired, weary and battered. 'A strange Turpin', they said.

There were more fights, some won, some lost, titles won and lost, and he finally retired after being knocked out by Yolande Pompey in Birmingham in September 1958.

By 1959 Turpin was broke and in debt. He and Gwen moved to a transport café in Russell Street, Leamington. Randolph did the cleaning and cooked for the lorry drivers. He also did a bit of wrestling, simply to help him pay his way. He worked for a while in George Middleton's scrapyard, and he sold his story to a Sunday newspaper for £1,000.

In 1961, Gwen gave birth to their third daughter, Charmaine, a sister to Gwyneth and Annette. In 1962, Randolph's stepfather, Ernest Manley, died and this was a great blow to all the Turpin family. It seemed to them as if this good and kindly man had always been there with them, and now he was gone.

A fourth daughter, Carmen, was born in 1964, and the money position was little short of desperate. So bad was it that Randolph decided to sell his trophies and his Lonsdale belt. But he just couldn't bring himself to do this and changed his mind at the last minute. He gave them to Gwen and advised her never to sell them. 'While you have these, you will always have a part of me,' he said.

Randolph had become bitter and full of hatred, blaming everyone else for the financial mess he found himself in. He hung a notice on the wall of his café: 'That which seldom comes back to him who waits is the money he lends to his friends'.

Although always generous, he had absolutely no sense of money at all. He spent it! He refused to listen to advice from anybody about money, about women or even about training.

Christmas 1965 and Randolph and Gwen spent the festive season with Jackie and Dick and their families. All seemed well and Randolph appeared quite happy, despite the fact that the Inland Revenue had filed a bankruptcy petition against him for £17,000 unpaid tax, and the Leamington Corporation had made a Compulsory Purchase Order on the café because they wanted the site for a car park.

The fateful day, 17th May 1966, started off in much the same way as all other days. Turpin was tidying and mopping up around the café, as he did every morning, and then, his chores completed, he sat down to write a letter. Gwen assumed the letter was to Beatrice, his mother, who was on holiday for a few days. Gwyneth and Annette had gone off to school and little Charmaine was being confined to her bed because she had a heavy cold. Carmen was then 17 months old, and was playing quite happily. After checking on Charmaine, Gwen went off to do a bit of shopping.

When she returned, everywhere seemed a little quiet. She put her purchases away and then went upstairs to look at Charmaine, whom she found deeply asleep. She went back downstairs, did a few more odd jobs, and then began to wonder where Randolph and baby Carmen had got to. She could not hear them. She went back upstairs, and then up the rather rickety stairs to the attic at the top of the house. All was quiet, and the door was shut. Gwen opened the door to be confronted with a fearsome sight. Carmen, covered in blood, was lying half off and half on the bed; Randolph lay in a crumpled heap upon the floor in a pool of blood so wide and deep it seemed almost to cover him.

Gwen screamed and, acting instinctively, gathered up the little girl and ran . . . and ran . . . and ran to the Warneford Hospital, fairly close by. There nursing staff gently broke the news that little Carmen had been shot!

When Gwen returned home, leaving her daughter in the care of the hospital, she found the police already in Russell Street, and they told her that Randolph was dead, shot, one bullet wound in his head and another in his chest. Carmen too had been shot twice, one bullet was lodged near her brain and a second had narrowly missed her heart, but had instead pierced a lung. All the shots were fired from a .22 calibre revolver found near the bodies.

Carmen, just a baby really, fought for her life and remained on the danger list for three weeks, while Gwen watched and prayed. The little girl won, though, and she survived.

The inquest was resumed in July. Gwen declared she knew nothing of the gun; she had never seen it, nor had Randolph ever spoken of owning one. It was confirmed that he had no licence for it, and the patholgist, Dr Derek Barrowcliff, said the gun was in poor mechanical condition.

Two letters were discovered; one to 'My dearest Gwen' and another, found in a kitchen drawer, apparently written some two years earlier. Gwen requested that the Coroner should have both letters read out, but apparently he decided this was inadvisable. There were too many names, he said.

It seems Randolph had been saying that he was being asked to pay tax on monies he had never received, and Mr George Middleton, Randy's manager, told the Coroner this was not true. He said he owed Randolph nothing, and that the boxer had received everything that was due to him.

Randolph had also talked wildy about a large sum of money being 'kept' for him, but had not given anybody any more details. He had also mentioned threats, and told of being beaten up by a 'gang of four hit men'. Gwen said he had returned home a bit bruised and battered at times, but she had asked no questions, merely assuming it was from wrestling. Randolph allowed her to go on thinking that. She said he had never, ever talked of taking his own life, even in their darkest days and with all their financial troubles.

The verdict was inevitable – that Randolph Turpin took his own life. There was no mention of 'balance of mind' and the inquest details are not available to the public for 75 years, ie the year 2041!

One or two boxing experts and sporting journalists, who considered Turpin to be one of the finest boxers Britain has ever produced, were very unhappy and puzzled by the inquest and its findings. They said that many questions were not asked, and many were not answered. The word 'whitewash' was used. Why had Randolph (apparently) shot baby Carmen? Where did the gun come from? Why had no one heard any shots, no one in the street, neighbours? There was no silencer on the gun, nor in the room. Did 'hit men' exist? If so, who were they and what were they after?

Was any money anywhere being kept for him, and if so by whom? Gwen said that he once telephoned someone and referred to this money, but she did not know to whom the call was made.

Turpin was buried in his home town of Leamington Spa, but not many sporting personalities or those from the boxing world turned up. The Vicar, the Rev Haselden, was quite scathing. He said, 'At the height of his career, Randolph was surrounded by those who regarded themselves as his friends and well wishers, but he was deserted by many when he lost his position and money.' This is both apt and true, but Randolph Turpin had been his own worst enemy and had refused all advice.

After the funeral a fund was started in Leamington aimed at helping Gwen and the children, but Gwen insisted that this should be stopped. She did not want any money; she said, 'We shall manage all right, thank you.'

And now, after being forgotten in his home town for years, Turpin's name has once more come to the fore.

In December 2000, Randolph Turpin's Lonsdale belt came up for auction for only the second time since the boxer's death. This belt was presented to him in 1956 after he had won the British Boxing Board of Control light-heavyweight championship of Great Britain for the third time. It is the last of the original belts, 9ct gold and still in its own original red leatherette case, with Turpin's name and details of the contests on both the belt and on its case.

Jackie Turpin, Randolph's only surviving brother, told the local newspaper, the *Leamington Courier*, that he believed the belt had passed to Randolph's eldest daughter, Gwyneth, after the tragedy of her father's death. Then he thought it had been sold by 'a friend of the family' in lieu of money he alleged Randolph owed him. Jackie said he didn't know the details and he had no idea who was putting the belt up for sale now. He said he would love to have been able to buy the belt himself, but it was financially impossible. He only hoped it would come back to the district where Randolph was born and bred. 'I'd love to be able to look at it and say "my brother won that",' he said.

Bidding for this famous belt waxed fast and furious and it was eventually knocked down to 'a lifelong friend and fan' for £23,000. The buyer, former Great Britain powerlifter and now Warwick businessman, Tony Baker, said that Turpin had always been an inspiration to him, and he intended 'bringing the belt back home'.

There is now a lifesize bronze statue of Randolph Turpin, commemorating the fiftieth anniversary of his 'greatest hour' – his win over Sugar Ray Robinson in July 1951 – erected in the Market Place at Warwick.

A PHANTOM FROM EDGEHILL

The late Brigadier Peter Young, scholar, soldier and military historian, published his definitive work *Edgehill 1642. The Campaign and the Battle* in 1967, touching but lightly upon the vexed subject of apparitions and ghostly manifestations. But as this battlefield, site of the first encounter of the English Civil War, is regarded as the most haunted battlefield in all England, he could scarcely *not* mention, albeit briefly, the great ghostly battle fought in the skies on the appropriate anniversary, the spectre of the white horse, the strange mists and goodness knows what else, all of which have been talked of, written about – and witnessed – for more than three hundred and fifty years.

He makes it quite clear, however, that although he has visited the site many times since he began his study of this conflict in 1935, he has not personally experienced any of the psychic phenomena associated with Edgehill. Nor for that matter anywhere else, he says. Perhaps jolly, bluff brigadiers do not make good 'hauntable material'.

It is not possible at the moment to get close to the actual site, nor for some years past. It is in the hands of the military and there is obviously much security. But as the Brigadier points out with great honesty, many people have spoken to him of the 'psychic aura' surrounding this spot. So he is assuming that to *some* people, *something* is there.

He makes time and space within the book to relate the very strange experiences of a visit in 1960 by Michael Howard Romney Woollard, better known as Michaeli, the famous concert pianist, who told his story himself to the Brigadier.

The view from Edgehill overlooking the battle area.

It seems that since childhood Michaeli had always had a vague sort of desire to visit this battlefield. He can in no way explain why this should be so. He has always had a sense of history. His own family, the Woollards, have been established in Suffolk since the 11th century and he was brought up with a sense of family history and tradition. But, so far he was able to discover, none of his family had anything to do with Edgehill. From ordinary school history lessons, he was well aware of the importance of this conflict, but how and why he should desire to visit the site, he cannot explain. He says he never had a wish to visit any battlefield anywhere other than Edgehill.

In June of 1960 an opportunity presented itself. Michaeli, in company with two friends, one of whom was a former Army officer, set off to pay his delayed visit to Edgehill. As they drove along Michaeli began to find the scenery, the landscape, oddly familiar although to his certain knowledge he had never in his life seen it before. Never been into this Midlands county. He found it all very curious and casually mentioned this to his companions, who seemed to find his observations amusing, taking them with a pinch of salt.

They drove on, but were eventually forced to a halt, since they had no idea which direction to take to head for the battle site. Michaeli, however, alighted from the car and looked about him. It was familiar, emphatically familiar, and with what he calls 'some instinct from the past' he was immediately able to direct the friend who was at the wheel to the exact spot which, at that time, lay more than two miles off.

Upon arrival at their destination, Michaeli and his friends were astounded to discover the whole place was now in the charge of the Army. They had no idea this was the case. They had honestly thought it would have been possible to set foot upon this famous bloody field. But it was not so.

Nothing daunted, Michaeli asked to see the officer in charge, and was escorted to his office. He told the officer he had come to fulfil the desire of his lifetime, to see this site, and he begged to be allowed to do so. At length the officer, who had listened sympathetically to all Michaeli said, was won over and was able to give his permission. And so the three friends set forth, but they had to be accompanied by armed soldiers with tracker dogs.

As they progressed Michaeli was beginning to feel apprehensive and when they approached a lane on the site, near to where it is known 'Roundheads and Cavaliers are buried together', a place now called 'Graveground Coppice', he became very agitated and disturbed. He said he felt many hundreds of eyes, all around and all watching him, their steady gaze never wavering. His two friends noticed he had become unwell, and he was obviously very frightened indeed. They asked him what was the matter, but all he could say to them was that he must go home immediately.

The party returned to London and Michaeli made his way to his own house alone. As he entered he was at once made aware of what he calls, with some feeling, a terrifying fact. He was *not* alone. He had brought back with him one of the dead from the bloody battlefield of Edgehill.

With great honesty, and in an attempt at explanation, he says that although he is not an adherent of spiritualism, which he describes as 'unnerving', he does accept that as an artist he lives, like most creative people, on a 'tauter plane of emotion', but these

The monument on the B4086 which commemorates the Civil War battle.

emotions must be kept under proper control, otherwise the artist cannot perform and certainly cannot perform in public.

He describes how this unwelcome visitor was unseen, but very evident, and accompanied him everywhere inside his house, from room to room. He saw him 'in my mind' and believed him to be a Roundhead; he wore armour and had a small moustache. His eyes were particularly deep and piercing and he carried a sword. His presence, always felt, always there, caused Michaeli much alarm. So much so, he was forced to keep the lights in all rooms burning throughout the night, and he only began to feel slightly less uneasy with the coming of day.

This man, whoever he was, remained for an entire month, and then suddenly he was gone, his departure as unexpected and as inexplicable as his arrival. Michaeli was left alone, in an extreme state of nerves, frightened and very unwell.

He had heard of the Society for Psychic Research, although he didn't know much about it, but he felt bound to write to them about his extraordinary experience. The Society replied that although they had much in their records about the haunted battlefield of Edgehill and all its ghostly manifestations, they could find nothing similar to this and they urged him to write everything down, carefully and with as much detail as he could muster.

Michaeli wonders if he had experienced a memory, transmitted through his ancient family, generation by generation, until it became so firmly planted in his mind that he was forced to visit an ancestor's scene of fear and conflict. Or, he asks, is there such a thing as reincarnation?

All he can state, he continues, is that this did take place; he did recognise the countryside; he did find he knew the way to the site; he was conscious, and fearful, of the hundreds of staring and unseen eyes; and he did return to his home accompanied by one whose intentions he felt to be malicious and unkindly. He concludes that all of this, the whole episode, was the most terrifying experience of his entire life, and that it will stay with him to the end of his days. Friends, he says, will confirm that he became very unwell while his uninvited guest remained, and that it took quite a long time after his departure for Michaeli to become his old self again.

He repeated this story to Brigadier Peter Young, when Young was engaged in research for his book. Michaeli's statement rests among Young's personal papers and a copy is in the hands of the Society for Psychic Research.

What happened to Michaeli is indeed a mystery. Why a spectre, a presence, from a long dead army should attach itself to one who, seemingly, has no connection whatsoever with Edgehill is a matter for conjecture; a riddle, insoluble on this side of the divide. But that is the way of ghosts.

THE LYNCHING OF
EDWARD BROME

It is quite astonishing that all the best ghost stories are said to follow on from events taking place around Christmastime. Perhaps it has something to do with the idea of the Roman festival held in mid-December, the 'Saturnalia'; or perhaps it is connected with the onset of the winter solstice. Maybe long dark nights provoke some people into carrying out long dark deeds!

Here in this story we have an eternal triangle of a sort, and a moral lesson in not leaping to conclusions. It was all of four centuries ago, and nothing much remains of the landscape of that age. The once wide open, bleak spaces have been taken over completely by encroaching suburbia, and it is extremely doubtful if any of the people living in the neat houses lining the modern roads of the housing estates in Keresley, on the edge of Coventry, will have heard of the tragedy. It isn't that the ghosts have gone away; it is just that life in this day and age is far too hectic to take them into account.

There was once a man called John Shore, a farmer in a fairly well to do way of business, and he had invited friends and neighbours to a 'bit of a do' at his home, Penny Park. He was a generous and hospitable host and so everybody was only too happy to accept his invitation. Shore was in love with the daughter of his neighbour, Sadler of Newlands Hall. Elizabeth was young and beautiful (aren't they all) and she was not without a copper or two. So he loved her, or said he did. We will be magnanimous and give him the benefit of the doubt.

Elizabeth was invited to the party. And so was another

neighbour, Edward Brome. A bit of a rascal this one, not averse to a touch of derring-do, but he also loved Elizabeth and wanted to marry her. Very obviously, Elizabeth's father favoured Shore. Much more suitable, much better match, and in general beneficial all round.

It was very likely that their betrothal was to be fixed this night, and was the real reason behind the celebration.

Elizabeth was riding, with a couple of servants, across the bleak and wintry landscape, en route for Penny Park when, suddenly, Brome rode up full pelt and stopped the little group dead in their tracks.

He pleaded his cause with the young Elizabeth; he pleaded most eloquently, but to no avail. She flatly refused to accompany him to his own house, not too far off; refused to elope; refused to run off. In short, refused him. Besides, Elizabeth was just a little flirty and flighty, and she wanted to go to Shore's party. Infuriated, Brome grabbed the bridle of her horse; a mild scuffle ensued, during which Elizabeth slid senseless to the ground. Her servants, terrified, picked her up and carried her inert body to John Shore's house.

When Shore saw his beloved Elizabeth lying deathly pale and unmoving, he was beside himself with rage. He believed it was that despicable rogue Edward Brome who had ended her life.

He called for horses and, accompanied by a couple of servants, he set off, hell for leather, to find and punish his adversary, to avenge the lovely Elizabeth. Brome had not gone far. He too thought he had killed Elizabeth; he was remorseful, devastated, and did not know what to do. He was wandering around on his horse, and his faithful hound trotted wherever his master led. He made no attempt at all to escape.

John Shore caught up with him and took him prisoner very easily. Shore spoke not a word, and heard not a word. Brome's devoted hound tried to protect his master, but Shore felled it with one hefty blow from his boot. They dragged Brome to a nearby barn and up into the loft, and they fastened a chain about his neck. This was the chain fixed in the loft, used to haul sacks of grain up into and down from the granary. So, amid thrashing around and general mayhem, Shore opened the trapdoor in the floor of the loft and gave Brome one mighty shove, to send him plunging to his death, as the chain tightened about his throat.

Sure that he had avenged his beloved, Shore rode back to his own house, honour satisfied. At least, he thought honour was satisfied. This honour business has never been especially clear to many of us, but there you are.

Upon his arrival in his own great hall, he was greeted by a happy and merry Elizabeth who, now fully recovered from her deathlike swoon, cast herself into his arms!

They covered up the story as best they could, with a whole pack of truly imaginative lies. They said Brome had been larking around in the barn, in a state of total inebriation, and had fallen accidentally through the trapdoor. They all said how shocked they were; what a shame; such a good chap too etc. The poor victim was buried, and Shore and his henchmen followed behind the coffin. Things died down. Just another nine days wonder.

Then the hauntings began. Brome and his hound were seen all over the place, particularly by those who had had a hand in his death, his murder, for murder it certainly was. It got that nobody would go to the house known as Penny Park, nor through Whitmore Park that surrounded it, after dark – even hardened travellers who would have used the road across the park, since it was by far the most convenient for them, reorganised their arrangements at the onset of dusk. One night, on the anniversary of the murder, a sceptical innkeeper accepted a wager to ride across the park and past the barn. He was found, mortally injured, in a ditch the following morning. His horse, lathered and trembling, turned up in Keresley two days later.

The hauntings became part of folklore. Newcomers were regaled with these stories, much embellished. In the natural course of things, lots of people moved into the area and, equally, lots moved out. Therefore, the telling and retelling became weakened.

In the 1930s a very wealthy businessman and benefactor, hailing from Coventry, moved into Penny Park, after spending a lot of his fortune turning it into a truly wonderful and comfortable home. It is believed that he resurrected the tales of hauntings. He claimed to have seen the spectre of Edward Brome on a path near the site of the death barn, clutching the fatal chain in his hand.

Well, there is nothing there now. Nothing is left of the barn, and if Edward Brome is still lurking, he must be moving around between the parked cars. And, you will be relieved to hear, he has been very quiet now for the best part of a hundred years.

Tragedy at Bedworth

This terrifying tragedy happened in peaceful Bedworth in June 1906, and the events leading up to it have remained a mystery ever since.

Bedworth, in the north of the county, was a close-knit mining community at that time. Most of its people worked in the mines; most lived in small terraced houses, and in close proximity so that they knew almost all there was to know about their neighbours. This proximity also enabled them to offer help to those self-same neighbours when it was needed. They were, in short, good, kind ordinary folk.

It was about twelve noon on Thursday, 14th June 1906, when people in the area were startled by the sound of two shots. They scarce had time to wonder about them when the air was rent by the sound of a third gunshot. The shots appeared to come from a group of tenement houses known as Thompson Buildings, in the Woodlands area of the town.

Neighbours immediately hastened in the direction of the shots and were stopped in their tracks when they found the body of a woman, 37 year old Mrs Louisa Cope, lying dead in the doorway of the house right next door to her own. Outside, in the communal yard, lay the body of 44 year old Walter Carter, the top of his head blown off by a double barrelled shotgun, with blood and pieces of flesh bespattering the surrounding brick walls and staining red the clothing on the line of washing, hanging out to dry in the sun.

An unnamed eye-witness spoke to the local newspaper, the *Nuneaton Chronicle*. He said he had seen Mrs Cope run from

Walter Carter's house, screaming. Carter was following with his shotgun. Desperate, Mrs Cope attempted to get into her own house, next door to that of Carter, but found her door closed. In a panic she ran to the house next door on the other side, occupied by a family named Walker. As she headed straight for the Walkers' door, Walter Carter lifted the gun and fired. His first shot missed Mrs Cope and hit the corner of an outhouse, bringing down a few bits of brick and mortar. The second shot, though, found Mrs Cope as she was about to enter the Walkers' house and reach safety. The bullet caught her in her back, but emerged, leaving a great gaping hole in her chest, and she fell to the ground, dead.

At this sight, Carter apparently halted and suddenly seemed to realise what had happened and what he had done. Quietly, he walked the few steps back to his front door. Equally quietly, and methodically, he emptied the cartridges from the breech of the shotgun and reloaded it. He then rested the stock upon the ground, laid his forehead over the end of the two barrels and, reaching down with one hand, pulled the trigger, blowing the top of his head clean off from above the eyebrows.

The eye-witness, understandably too stunned to move at first, then ran to a nearby green field where he fell down, burying his face in the cool green grass, and was violently sick.

What on earth had happened to cause Walter Carter to murder his neighbour and then, in horror at what he had done, blow his own brains out?

Walter Carter, a miner at nearby Newdigate Colliery, was described as a tall man who wore a shade over one eye, having lost an eye in a mining accident some years previously. By all accounts, he was well liked and respected. He was on good terms with everybody, did not drink and, according to his own children, never got into a passion. His son declared the only time he recalled his father becoming angry was when he, the son, was a youngster and was discovered playing truant from school. Walter Carter's only extra-mural activity was the cultivation of his allotment – altogether a totally blameless life.

At the time of the shooting, Carter had been a widower for some seven years. There were seven children of his marriage; four of them had left home, while the remaining three still lived with their father.

Mrs Louisa Cope lived with her husband William, a bricklayer by trade, and her two illegitimate children, a girl aged 18 and a boy of 15. The Copes had been married in Birmingham and were just about to celebrate their eighth wedding anniversary. William Cope was not the father of Mrs Cope's children, but seems to have accepted them and had no problems being a stepfather to them. Cope described his wife as an even-tempered woman, always joking, and said she did not drink. They all lived together comfortably, he declared. They regarded the Carter family as friends and also got on well with the Walkers, Martha and Alfred, their other neighbours.

It seems that Walter Carter had been having a bit of a hard time. Two of his children were still at school and he was working varying shifts at the colliery. In those days you didn't argue about shifts, but did as you were told. Therefore he was finding it difficult to manage the household, so Mrs Cope agreed to come in and 'do' for him. This arrangement continued for some time and Louisa spent much of her day in the Carter house, although William Cope was very careful to point out that she did not in any way neglect her own home in the process.

Then, some weeks prior to the tragedy, the Copes took in a lodger, Joseph Anderton. He worked alongside Walter Carter at Newdigate Colliery, doing mine timbering, and the two men appeared to get on well together. Anderton described Walter Carter as his friend and said they often walked over to the allotments together.

Then William Cope decided his wife was working too hard. The extra work occasioned by the taking in of a lodger, plus work in the Carter home and looking after her own house and family as well, was making her ill, he said. He told her she must give up the Carter household; she must tell Walter she could no longer go in and help him. But another six weeks went by and the situation remained exactly as it was before. Cope then asked his wife if she had indeed told Carter he must find someone else to look after his house, and she declared she had done so. She told William that

Carter had asked her to go down to 'the Union' and see if she could find a suitable woman who would come in and do a bit of cleaning. But, despite William Cope's instructions, Louisa did not do this, instead continuing to go every day to the Carter household.

Reading between the lines, it would seem that William Cope was rapidly losing patience with the situation, and before he left for work on that fateful Thursday morning, he once again issued his ultimatum, telling Louisa she must give up helping in the Carter house; she must tell Carter to find someone else to take on the job and she must concentrate on her own home. William Cope never saw his wife alive again.

Alfred Walker, next door, said he knew both families very well. He knew Mrs Cope helped out in the Carter household; he agreed he 'might have heard little questions' but he took no notice of them. He minded his own business and he had never seen any improper conduct between them.

On the day prior to the tragedy, Walker and Carter had been chatting to some other men down on the allotments. Carter had rested himself, leaning on his spade, and had spoken of 'having a little bother' with Mrs Cope. He had declared he expected it would be a 'bigger bother' yet and had told the men that if they wanted anything out of his house, they could have it, for everything was for sale.

Walter Carter had also told Joseph Anderton he was 'having a bit of bother with Mrs Cope' but Anderton had not known what he was talking about and, not wanting to become involved in neighbour problems in any way, he had merely shrugged off the issue and advised Carter to 'take no notice'.

Mrs Martha Walker, wife of Alfred, was friendly with her next door neighbour, Louisa Cope. She said Louisa had told her she could no longer manage the chores of the Carter household and that her husband was firmly insisting she give it up. But, she said, Walter Carter had threatened to 'blow her brains out' if she didn't continue to turn up.

Carter's eldest son, also named Walter, his eyes red with prolonged weeping and still obviously in a state of shock at the time of the inquest, said he knew of nothing at all improper between his father and Mrs Cope, although he said 'there was more than ordinary duty' between them and they seemed very affectionate towards one another. His father had given Mrs Cope small gifts and had taken her on a trip to the seaside, although Mr Cope had accompanied them. He had never seen his father put his arms around Mrs Cope; nor kiss her; nor ever call her anything other than 'Mrs Cope'.

He knew of no bother until very early on the morning of the shooting. He was asleep in bed, having been on the night shift at the colliery, and he was awakened by loud talk, but took little or no notice and went back to sleep. The next thing he heard was the gunshots. The gun belonged to his father and had always been kept in the house, he declared.

The Coroner said that the double tragedy was incomprehensible, the evidence he had heard gave no apparent reason for it and the motive was 'past finding out'.

The inquest jury returned a verdict of murder by Walter Carter on the death of Louisa Cope, and a verdict of *felo de se* (suicide) on Walter Carter's own death. It was, of course, the only possible verdict in the circumstances.

However, the verdict of *felo de se* in respect of Walter Carter upset the funeral arrangements made by his family, for it meant his body had to be buried during the hours of darkness, within 24 hours of the inquest and without Christian ceremony of any kind. So, the rough coffin was carried on a plain wagonette, drawn along by the undertaker himself, taken to the cemetery at dark of night and very speedily interred. The cemetery gates were then locked in order to keep the curious away.

The following Monday, Mrs Louisa Cope was buried and the local newspaper reported some 'uncreditable' incidents. Several people had shouted 'Hooray'; one woman had danced an impromptu jig; and a musical instrument (not specifically described) had been played, apparently inappropriately. At the graveside, disrespectful remarks had been bandied about, and once again the cemetery gates were kept locked.

Since Walter Carter was seen to commit the murder and then

turn the gun upon himself, obviously there was no murder trial. It is also customary for the Coroner at any inquest to attempt to spare the feelings of the deceased person's relatives, to stifle any malicious gossip and to stem the tide of speculation when to do otherwise would serve no useful purpose and no public good.

The whole business of the shooting was, as far as the inquest was concerned, perfectly clear. It was the reason for it, the motive, that baffled all and sundry. That is, unless there was much more to the relationship between Louisa Cope and Walter Carter than met the eye, and more than any of those questioned would admit to knowing about. Was Carter jealous of Mrs Cope's new lodger, whose recent arrival seemed likely to deprive him of her attentions to his own household? Did he think that perhaps Louisa Cope looked with a certain warmth upon Joseph Anderton?

Why was Mrs Cope's funeral turned into a bit of a circus? In the light of such an appalling tragedy, it would seem more likely, more natural, that the neighbourhood would feel pity and compassion, but instead there were jeering remarks and even sneers. Most people try to behave with some vestige of respect when someone dies and is buried, even if they had not been very close, or even liked them much. This applies even in our present cynical age and way back in 1906, when people stood still in the street and men took off their hats as the cortege passed, it was even more so. So, the question arises, why the disrespect for Louisa Cope?

Was it perhaps the manifestation of the ancient rite of 'rough music' or the 'skimmetty ride' as used by Thomas Hardy in *The Mayor of Casterbridge*? In this, persons involved in adulterous liaisons were carried through the streets in effigy, and then the effigies were burned, all to a great deal of noise made by the banging of pots and pans. This let the adulterous couple know that their neighbours were well aware of what was going on! 'Rough music' continued in Warwickshire for quite a long time.

Or did they just dislike Mrs Cope? And if so, why?

According to witnesses, both Louisa Cope and Walter Carter were perfectly ordinary, friendly people, who never had a cross word with anyone. But either they were both consummate actors or those near to them were simply not telling the entire truth – for this just could not be. Walter Carter must have been in a most fearful state of mind when he shot Mrs Cope as she ran from him; to fire twice at her, then turn the gun upon himself. This is not the work of an 'ordinary' person. There simply must have been undercurrents, albeit unknown or unacknowledged.

Why didn't Mrs Cope simply tell Walter Carter she could no longer continue to perform his household chores? Why didn't she try to find another woman to work for him? In 1906, a few extra shillings per week would have been very acceptable to a lot of women, so this would have been easy to achieve. But Mrs Cope seemingly made no endeavour to look for someone else.

If indeed, as the inquest was told, the relationship was merely that of a kindly neighbour helping out a widower, she could have told Carter enough was enough and he would have had to have accepted it. Instead, there were two dreadful and tragic deaths. Louisa must have said something to Carter and this might have been the 'bit of bother' about which Carter spoke to his mates on the allotments. It is unbelievable that Louisa Cope died because she wanted to give up her job. It is much more likely that she had begun to transfer her affections. But none of this came to light, and now we must accept that the solution to the mystery may never be known.

THE CLERIC IN
THE COFFIN

When you walk along the Victoria Embankment in London you are walking on a bit of Warwickshire. A very little bit! For the cement used here came from the Warwickshire village of Stockton, built upon one of its vital ingredients, blue lias limestone.

Another thing for which Stockton is famous is one of the most extraordinary and eccentric clerics of all time. Warwickshire has had, through the ages, some quite unusual clergymen, but the behaviour of the Venerable Archdeacon Colley, Rector of the church of St Michael and All Angels at Stockton, in January 1912 really does take a bit of swallowing. It certainly stunned his congregation into a silence slightly tinged with fear.

It was Evensong, and there had been absolutely nothing at all untoward within the service. Canon Colley had taken as his text 'Set thine house in order; for thou shalt die, and not live' (II Kings). There followed his own adaptation of 'The Angelic Ascription' (Revelations) set to Mozart's beautiful Twelfth Mass. Moving over to the music desk – a particular feature of this church – the Canon faced the large congregation and made the following extraordinary announcement.

'Since I do not feel that I am getting any younger, I have had my coffin – which many of you for eight years have known I had made for me – brought over from the Rectory, and it now stands before you in the chancel. In the year 1904 (on the 14th May) I left my body to the University of Birmingham, for the use of medical students and to be cut up in the interests of anatomical

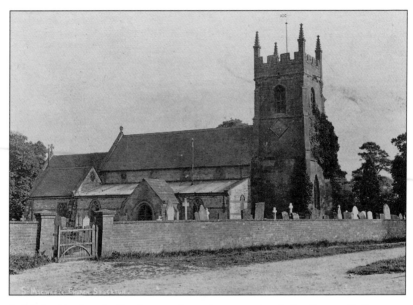

St Michael's church, Stockton, where the eccentric cleric, Canon Colley, was rector. (Warwickshire Record Office – PH 350/2068)

and surgical science when I have done with it.'

Having got thus far, the Canon called for what he termed his 'bearers' to come forward. Still clothed in cassock, surplice, stole and hood, he stepped into the coffin which had been reared upon its end. The lid, made of glass, was fixed over him and the coffin lowered to a horizontal position. The four bearers grasped the four handles and slowly carried the coffin up the aisle, towards the west door, turned around and came back again. The coffin was borne about waist high so that the congregation could see the very much still alive body and features of their rector as he passed them. Some were horrified and fearful; others considered it to be a blasphemous mockery of death itself and hastily left the church. Some were spellbound, shaken into a fearful numbness, whilst others, overcome by emotion, burst into sobs. One or two, well used to Canon Colley's foibles and idiosyncrasies, giggled hysterically.

His little trip over, the coffin was once more stood up on its end, the glass lid removed and the Canon assisted to alight. He was heard to remark, 'For this relief much thanks.'

He then, seemingly impervious to the consternation he had caused, wished everyone a happy new year, and in thankfulness for the mercies of the year just past they all sang (or those who remained) *Praise God from whom all blessings flow*. Then came the Benediction, as usual, and the remainder of the worshippers filed out swiftly, probably glad to be off back home, away from such bizarre antics and amid things ordinary and normal.

Word of these goings-on got about and the local newspaper sent a reporter to interview Canon Colley, who was more than ready to explain his actions. He said he wished to impress upon his congregation, by the object lesson of Sunday last, his absolute conviction with regard to what he had always taught. He quoted the Latin adage *mors janua vitae* – death is the gate of life. This was no new idea of his, he went on. Most of his parishioners knew of it, and he merely wished to have a rehearsal so that when he died there would be no need for delay in carrying out his wishes to leave his body, since he would now have finished with it, for the use of science. He desired that it should be very promptly handed over. To this end, he had already made arrangements with all the authorities likely to be involved.

He produced, with a flourish and to emphasise his point, a copy of a letter he had sent to the Faculty of Medicine, Birmingham University, in 1904. This read:

Since seeing you about the disposal of my body for dissection, I have made my will, an extract from which is herein enclosed. Also I have now ready a box, on the lid of which directions are printed to ensure that my remains placed therein shall, with all possible speed, be carried by four of my parishioners to the University of Birmingham. I should therefore be glad if you would kindly suggest what had further best be written to guide those who may have to see to this when I have breathed my last.

As when a child I was laid out for dead and narrowly

escaped being buried alive (my son Captain Colley of the Royal Artillery knows of this, having been told of it by my father, his grandfather) and fearing the same danger might recur under like circumstances and trance, I therefore ask that before making dissection it may be seen that I am really dead.

Please again tell me what I should do about giving in a letter or other formal disposal of my mortal remains, to be brought under my hand with my coffined corpse, particulars of what I should write as to mental idiosyncrasies, line of thought, bend of disposition, bias of will, likes and dislikes, with whatever else may be useful when the top of my skull, as we arranged, shall be sawn off, to enable exploration to be made, that it may be known if I am, or have been, any more mad than other people.

The Canon went on to ask if the University would do all the arranging, at a cost to be borne by his estate, and requested that they would wire his bones together as a skeleton, labelled as directed, and have this placed in the Psychic Museum in Leamington. Alternatively, his bones could be kept safely and handed over to his son when he returned to England from India. The Canon said his son knew of and approved all these plans and arrangements.

The reply to this lengthy missive was reassuring. Dr William Wright of the Faculty of Medicine wrote that he thought the Canon had fully understood all that was required. He asked that upon the Canon's death a letter should be sent to the Dean of the Faculty, and the body should be sent to the same address. He promised to make sure the Canon *was dead* and he said a letter regarding the Canon's temperament could be sent to him. He signed off 'Trusting you are well' and then, in brackets, added 'That's funny isn't it?' Well, it was really!

The Canon then got busy with a whole set of further instructions. Immediately upon his death, his body was to be put into the coffin which he had prepared; it was to be taken up by four strong men, carried to the railway station and despatched to the University of Birmingham. He wished his body to be attired in the canonicals – the cassock, surplice, stole and hood – which he had always worn as Rector of Stockton. The four bearers were each to be given one pound for railway expenses.

This does conjure up for us a very odd picture indeed. Imagine four strong men, soberly clad, somberly hatted and gloved, struggling to cart a glass-topped coffin into the local railway station. The Canon, dressed in accordance with his own instructions, would be perfectly visible beneath his glass to all passengers, porters and ticket collectors! He would then be pushed onto the train, probably with difficulty, and chugged towards Birmingham with that wonderful sound that all steam engines made. Could all this be remotely possible? Perhaps in the Canon's days, but assuredly not today.

He further instructed that a telegram should be sent to his son, Clifton Colley, then in India. He had prepared it, all ready for transmission when the time came.

Just going forward for a little rest in the beyond before seeking another incarnation. Shall try to let you know of my occasional presence. Have left instructions as we together arranged. Body in box, just going to medical faculty of Birmingham University. Hurrah for next innings, a round we trust of useful life.
Your loving father.

'You see,' the Archdeacon firmly told the by now bewildered reporter, 'I hope and expect that after death and a spell of rest – which may be one year or five hundred – I shall return again for useful work. This is a doctrine I believe and have always taught.' He paused for thought and then, in measured response to a further question, he said, 'Yes, I suppose I may hear something from the Bishop. We shall just have to wait and see. . .'

It would seem that Canon Colley was not at all a miserable man, dwelling upon death. He was brisk, quite jolly and very fond of music. He described himself as a Graduate of Music although he gave no details of where he graduated from!

He was a keen student of spiritualism and also very keen on repentance (quite a usual thing for a clergyman of 1912) and he wrote a pamphlet purporting to be the *History of Stockton Parish Church*, describing the symbolism of the 'Devil's door'. This is apparently the name given to the north door of any church, since it faces a colder atmosphere than, say, a south door. Being colder, this is the side the Devil prefers to linger, lying in wait for sinners who shun the paths of righteousness.

So, what finally happend to the Canon? His end was indeed a mystery. Perhaps he did hear from his Bishop after the theatricals with the coffin, for he resigned the living of Stockton in February 1912, just one month later. He remained in the Warwick/ Leamington region for a while longer and was then discovered in Middlesborough, Teeside. But doing what? His name appears in no directories; he had no parish there; his name occurs in no newspaper reports. But he died there, very suddenly, in October 1912.

Enquiries at the University of Birmingham yield nothing, for all records of that period, and indeed most pre-Second World War records, are gone forever, destroyed by bombs, by fire and ultimately by purposeful incineration due to lack of storage space. Whether they ever received the body in its glass-topped coffin we shall never know. Nor shall we ever know what they might have discovered if they had begin to dissect it.

A much later report (1987) in the *Leamington Courier* says simply that Canon Colley died suddenly in Middlesbrough and was cremated in due course. So his last wishes – for his bones to be wired together as a skeleton – were never carried out.

Did he allow his son – or indeed anybody else – to become aware of his 'occasional presence', one wonders? If so it has never been reported. It would have been good to discover what exactly happened in the end to Stockton's eccentric cleric.

THE DEATH OF MISS MARY

It is astonishing to those of us who are amateur criminologists to realise just how sophisticated police technology has rapidly become. No one now even glances upwards at the sound of a police helicopter, and yet in 1968, when the police used such a machine for the first time in Warwickshire, to mount a fair sized manhunt around the village of Henley-in-Arden, we all thought it quite wonderful. And it was successful in helping to find the perpetrator of a brutal murder.

The victim was 46 year old Miss Mary Helen Joyce Hutchinson, who lived with her elderly parents, Cecil Hutchinson, aged 80, and his wife Ada, aged 78. The Hutchinsons' home was a very comfortable bungalow called The Rosary, at Preston Bagot, a couple of miles outside Henley-in-Arden, and they had been there for 40 years. Their son, Eric, had married and moved away, but not very far, just to Coleshill, and the whole family, the four of them, were devoted to and very supportive of each other.

Daughter Mary had never married, but she was most certainly not the timid spinster type. She was a career woman, and had worked her way up to a senior managerial position in a Henley firm. She was good at her job, well known and respected throughout the area and was greatly admired by a lot of people who knew her well. Locals referred to her simply as 'Miss Mary'.

Henley-in-Arden and its immediate environs now tend to sprawl somewhat, but way back in 1968 the sprawl had not quite begun. Most of the residents knew each other and each other's families, many of whom had been rooted there for generations. They knew habits and foibles; and they had known Miss Mary since she was a child.

Mary Hutchinson, with rabbits for the pot. (Warwickshire Constabulary)

She was born in March 1922 and went to school in Henley until 1937, when she left and obtained a job as a clerk with a local bakery firm. But Miss Mary had ambitions, albeit quite modest ones, and in the old fashioned jargon of those times, she wanted to 'better herself'. She went to night school to obtain more qualifications, and she applied her enormous energy and firm-mindedness to this end.

The war intervened in her life, as it did in the lives of so many people, and from October 1942 until July 1946, Miss Mary served in the Royal Signals branch of the Women's Auxiliary Service. After her 'demob' and her return to home life, she resumed her employment until 1955, when she obtained a new job with a locally based firm, Abrasive Developments. She worked very hard, and was obviously a woman of initiative, for she moved steadily upwards from a fairly junior post to managership of one of the company's divisions. To Mary Hutchinson her work was her whole life, she loved it, lived it, and thought really of little else.

She did do a bit of voluntary work upon occasions, but apart from the odd visit to friends and relatives, she seems to have had little social life, nor did she appear to want it. She was said to be a very kind lady, but not particularly good at mixing.

She travelled extensively in connection with her work and both her employers and her colleagues held her in high regard.

Mary Hutchinson loved the countryside and enjoyed solitary walking. One of her foibles was to walk to work every morning. She had a car and there was absolutely no reason why she could not drive there, but for her each day began with a two mile walk – fresh air and exercise. No matter what the weather, Mary Hutchinson set off across the fields that skirted The Mount, formerly the site of an ancient motte and bailey castle. She wore wellington boots and kept a pair of shoes at the office to change into upon her arrival.

Everyone knew this was her inveterate practice, and upon more than one occasion colleagues at work joked with her saying, 'Someone will jump out at you one of these days. . .' Miss Mary merely grinned and replied, 'I am too big and too ugly for anyone to want to. . .'

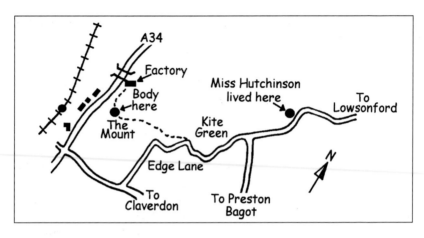

Miss Hutchinson's route to the factory where she worked took her along the lane to Kite Green and then on to a footpath (dotted line) across the fields.

At about 7.50 am on 28th August 1968, all was as usual and Miss Mary set off on her two mile walk to work. She had a lot to think about, for her firm – and in particular her division – was involved in a revolutionary chemical pioneering process.

But Mary Hutchinson never arrived at her work.

This rather surprised her colleagues, but then someone remembered that a former employee of the firm had died and was to be buried on that day. Mary Hutchinson had wondered aloud whether she ought to attend the funeral, but had then decided she would not do so. When she did not turn up, it was thought she had changed her mind and decided to attend the funeral after all.

But there was no word from her, and this was not at all like her. They expected she would have sent a message and let them know what time she would be coming into work. By mid-morning when there was still no word, one of the staff decided that, as he had to go out in the direction of The Rosary, he would just call in briefly and make sure Mary was not ill. But when he arrived he found the house empty. Mr and Mrs Hutchinson, having seen their daughter off to work as usual, had decided to treat themselves to a day out shopping and there was no one at home.

Miss Mary didn't come home at the usual time, but this did not unduly bother her parents. She sometimes stayed on a bit, working late. Her colleagues thought Mary was at home; her parents assumed she was at work; so the alarm was not raised until the following morning when it was realised she had not been home all night.

Cecil Hutchinson enlisted the aid of a former neighbour, and they set off on the route they knew Mary always took to work – and it was they who found her murdered body.

She was lying grotesquely in a grassy hollow at the foot of The Mount, a hollow that in spring was filled with bluebells. The body was covered over with grass and nettles, and the searchers might not have found it at all had it not been for a curious cow who was seeking greener grass and in doing so had nudged aside the concealing loose vegetation. Mary had been strangled. Her clothing was torn and disarranged and this gave rise to the idea that she had been sexually assaulted, but the post mortem revealed this was not the case.

Near to the body they found the holdall she usually had with her, but there was no sign of the handbag in which she invariably carried cash and her cheque book. This was found sometime later, about a mile off, lying near a disused railway line, and of course, it was empty.

At the top of the hill above the hollow police noticed signs that someone had been sleeping rough. There were crumpled and obscure magazines, food bags and a ballpoint pen lying on the ground.

House to house enquiries were begun and an incident room was quickly established in a local hall, while the WRVS struggled to produce their quota of meals on wheels from the adjacent room.

The weekend following the murder was Henley-in-Arden's carnival weekend – an annual event requiring much organisation, much work and much preparation. It was invariably well attended and greatly looked forward to. In this year, however, it had an unusual addition. A police float, with loud speaker, requesting anyone who had seen anything unusual, had noticed or knew of a person or persons sleeping rough on The Mount, to please come forward with the information. On the Sunday, at church, the Vicar advised all women to be extra vigilant and not to venture out alone.

A total of seven hundred and fifty statements were taken; fifty of these were from tramps and vagrants who admitted passing through Henley-in-Arden. It was in no way unusual for a vagrant to sleep rough on The Mount, and some of the shops in Henley reported that such strangers had bought food around the time in question. But none of this really led anywhere much.

The police helicopter was brought in to scan the area for signs of anyone sleeping rough, indeed for signs of anything. And it was from the helicopter that a tarpaulin was spotted. This had been reported taken from a nearby farm, but the vagrant himself, who had apparently stolen it to wrap himself in whilst asleep at night, was nowhere to be seen.

It was thought that the unknown vagrant must have been familiar with the area and might well also have known of Miss Mary's practice of walking across the fields to her work each morning. It was evident that he knew his way up and down The Mount, but despite diligent enquiries it was not until the following month that the police got a breakthrough. More than a hundred police officers had spent the intervening time combing the brush and scrub on and around the whole area of The Mount.

Leonard Peter Ruff, a 34 year old, 18 stone, unemployed labourer, was released after a two year term in Winson Green prison, Birmingham, just six days before Mary Hutchinson was murdered. When the investigation was in full cry, a fellow inmate came forward with the information that in prison Ruff had talked of Henley-in-Arden and had spoken of a 'woman company director' who, he thought, 'could well have a bit of poke in her handbag.'

In September, Ruff was caught breaking and entering a cafe at Evesham and was promptly arrested. He mentioned having slept rough at Henley-in-Arden recently and eventually confessed to the murder of poor Mary Hutchinson.

Ruff was born at Temple Grafton, near Stratford-upon-Avon, in 1933. Just before his birth, his sister Dorothy was burned to death in the family home when her dress caught fire. While Ruff was still a small child, his brother Bill was drowned whilst swimming in a local pond with one of his schoolmates. When Leonard Ruff was only 9 years old, his mother became very ill, had to undergo a serious operation and died, leaving the youngster alone with his father in the cottage at Temple Grafton.

When he left school, Ruff took work as a labourer on a local farm, but this came to an abrupt end when his employer's wife was found with serious neck wounds. Ruff was charged with unlawful wounding and put on probation for three years.

He was called up for National Service in 1952 and seems to have done quite well whilst in the Army, where he learned the trade of a blacksmith. He told friends it might have suited his build, but it didn't suit his temperament and he didn't really like it much. He was discharged from the Army with a conduct rating of 'very good' and when he returned to his home he obtained work with the (then) Alcester Rural District Council as a gang man.

Then his father died shortly after, leaving the Temple Grafton cottage and its contents, together with his modest savings, to his son – his only surviving child. Ruff lost no time in smashing every stick of furniture in the place before putting the cottage on the market. It was said to be a 'symbolic severing' of all the unhappy links with his past.

The money he got from the sale of the cottage, plus his father's savings, was very soon all dissipated by betting on the horses. Once again, Ruff was penniless – and he took to crime. At this stage it was mostly petty thievery, just small sums of money. He was invariably caught and often just gave himself up. He appears to have had a strange respect for Authority (with a capital 'A') for not only did he behave well whilst in the Army, but also during his several terms in prison, and he always achieved the one-third remittance for good conduct.

When Ruff was charged with the murder of Miss Mary, his aunt, Mrs May O'Dell, who still lived in Temple Grafton, was absolutely astounded. She just could not believe it. She told the local newspaper, 'He wouldn't hurt a fly, big as he is. . .' She described him as a shy man. 'Always a loner,' she said. 'Big as he

was as a schoolboy, he's always run from older boys. He wouldn't
hurt a fly. . .'

Leonard Peter Ruff appeared before Warwick Assizes in
January 1969 and pleaded guilty to the murder of Miss Mary
Hutchinson the previous August. In his statement to police, Ruff
said, 'I was walking up The Mount when I saw this woman. I
stopped her and said, "I have been locked away for two years and
no one wants to know me. . ." She said, "You do look lonely." My
mind went blank, and I grabbed her. She said, "Please don't hurt
me. God will help you." I felt her go limp.'

He continued, 'I have no friends and nobody wants to know
me. It was not for sex; it was not for gain. When I killed her I just
wanted to get revenge on . . . somebody. . .'

What kind of revenge and for what, perhaps he did not know
himself. The whole of his life had been marred by tragedy. The
symbolic destruction of the bits-and-pieces of his home, a place of
great unhappiness for him, seems appallingly significant. He was a
loner, who was also desperately lonely, and he just couldn't cope
with it.

The trial was over very quickly. The Judge concluded: 'This was
a senseless killing. It is tragic that this good lady should end in this
fashion.'

Ruff maintained a passive countenance as he stood to hear the
Judge sentence him to life imprisonment. Indeed, according to
reports in the local press, his facial expression had scarce altered
throughout the proceedings, and he showed no sign of emotion as
he was led away, back to the cells, to be locked up for many, many
years.

BLOODSTAINED BIRD SEED

On a misty November night in 1974 a retired café owner, Jack Taylor, was found brutally stabbed to death in the hallway of his own home. Beside him lay his little dog and their bloody and battered bodies rested upon half a hundredweight of bloodstained bird seed!

The frenzied killing of this harmless, very well liked and respected widower and his pet dog, his companion of many years, shocked and horrified the town of Warwick where almost everyone knew him.

Jack Taylor, with his slightly portly build and his sandy-greying hair was a popular figure. He was involved in many sporting activities and until his retirement had run a café in West Street, Warwick, a noted rendezvous for lorry drivers the length and breadth of the country. As they collected and delivered from north to south, east to west, and vice versa, almost all had to come through the centre of England and 'See you in Old Jack's in Warwick' became a catchphrase among them. Jack Taylor served plain and ample fare, exactly what hungry lorry drivers with not too much time to spare needed. His business thrived.

Taylor was a Geordie, born in South Shields in 1909, and he still retained traces of his native accent. For some 22 years he served in the Merchant Navy as a Chief Steward, and he continued in the Merchant Navy through the Second World War. When he left the service, he married. His bride, Doreen Prosser, had been married before and had one child, a daughter, Sylvia. However, little is known of Sylvia. As she reached adulthood, she grew away from the family. She left home after a quarrel and disappeared from the lives of the Taylors.

Three children were born to Jack and Doreen, John in 1946, Alan in 1947 and Jennifer in 1948. It was shortly after the end of the war; things had not got better, nor returned to normal, as quickly as people had hoped and housing accommodation was practically non-existent. Jack had a widowed sister, Isobel, living in Handsworth, Birmingham, and the Taylor family made their home with her for the time being. It seems Isobel truly welcomed them and the whole family were happy together and very supportive of each other.

Both Jack and Doreen worked in the catering trade in Birmingham at the Civic Restaurant and then later at Tamworth Race Track. Isobel helped with the care of the growing children, but eventually the Taylors decided it was time for them to strike out on their own. Round about Christmastime in 1954, Jack Taylor took on the lease of what was then known as Readings Café at 62 West Street, Warwick.

This was a courageous venture, but according to his son Alan, his parents had talked much about running their own business. It was a dream and an ambition and when Readings Café came up, it was an opportunity not to be missed. The premises were in a good position and had the added attraction of living accommodation upstairs, with ample room for three growing youngsters. Jack and Doreen both worked long hours to build up trade, and they prospered, as indeed they deserved to do.

Eventually, it became possible for Jack to buy the café and when John and Alan left school, they went into the business with him. But it was not long before Alan decided he was too young to settle down, and he really longed to see something of the world. Knowing of his father's Merchant Navy life, he joined that service as a galley boy, but after some 18 months, he deserted in New Zealand and remained in that far-off country for more than a year.

In 1964, Doreen Taylor became desperately ill and Jack Taylor wrote to his son in New Zealand asking him to come home and see his mother before she died. Alan immediately gave himself up to the New Zealand authorities as a deserter and was deported back to this country, arriving on 6th August, just in time to spend a few last days with his mother before she died on 13th August.

After Doreen's death, Alan stayed on for a while. His father was grief stricken. After all the years he and Doreen had been together and worked together, her death really knocked him over. Both Alan and John helped in the café, but ultimately, inevitably, there was a quarrel. Not a very serious one, not over anything very important, and Alan could not even remember what it was about. But both he and his brother John, young and possibly a bit hasty, left and went to seek work elsewhere. By this time, their sister Jennifer had already left and was training to be a beautician in London. Therefore, for the first time in many years, Jack Taylor was alone; living alone and running his business alone.

However, some 18 months or so later, both sons returned, patched up the quarrel and were once again helping to run the business alongside their father.

Both sons knew full well their father had relationships with other women after Doreen's death, but neither of them regarded any of them as even remotely serious. So Jack sought solace in his loneliness; so what? They were glad he had friends and they both knew with absolute certainty that Jack had no intention of ever re-marrying.

In 1970, Alan was again getting itchy feet and wanted to go to sea, but his attempts were unsuccessful. The family business was not as thriving as it had once been. Things change. New roads had been built and there was a bypass and other routes for the delivery of goods rather than struggling through the Warwick town traffic. With all this, Jack's café lost a considerable amount of trade and it no longer made enough to keep them all. Alan took other jobs, but his brother John became very ill with a nervous breakdown, which caused the family, and especially Jack, much anxiety.

A couple of years later, Jack Taylor decided enough was enough. He would get out while the going was good and while he was still of an age when he could enjoy his retirement. He received what he considered a fair price for the business and he bought a small house for himself at 100 Stratford Road, about a mile down the road from the café. A neat house, on a corner plot, with a nice bit of garden. Jack decided he would buy himself a greenhouse, do a bit of real gardening and concentrate on his hobby – canaries. Jack was a recognised authority on canary breeding, nationally known and very successful. He had been a member of the Cage Birds Society for years and attended all their functions. He bred from his own prize birds. Sometimes he would sell, but not very often – he liked them a bit too well to part with them.

In 1974, Jennifer married and Jack travelled to the United States to attend his daughter's wedding in Los Angeles. John was also in the States at that time and was working his way around the country.

Alan met a girl called Claire Holtom and together they set off to travel the world, hippie fashion, working their passage, taking on any jobs and moving from country to country. It was the 'thing to do' in that period. But eventually, they both wanted to come home and they returned to Warwick to stay for a while with Jack while they sorted themselves out. They took a caravan at Bloxham near Banbury. Alan worked at Banbury Post Office, while Claire, a nurse, got a job at Banbury Hospital. They visited Jack every week without fail and Alan telephoned his father regularly between visits.

Although Jack Taylor lived alone, he was far from being a lonely man. He was very active; went out a lot; had many friends, who often dropped in on him. He enjoyed going to his local for a drink and frequently attended sporting events and social functions. And there were his canaries!

He was due to attend an important canary show in Oxford on 15th November 1974. It was arranged that Alan and Claire should accompany him, for a day out, and then Jack would return to Bloxham with them for the evening.

It was Alan's habit to telephone his father on Wednesdays, but on 13th November, he knew Jack would not be at home, because he was to attend the Midland Sporting Club dinner in Solihull, with friends. So Alan telephoned the following day, Thursday 14th, but could get no reply. He didn't bother too much about it, merely assuming Jack had gone out. He phoned several times, but got no answer.

On Friday 15th, Jack simply did not turn up at Bloxham. They waited for him and telephoned several times, but no reply. Eventually, Alan made a last phone call from a telephone box in Bloxham at around 11 o'clock on the Friday night, and when he still did not get any reply, and his father had not turned up anywhere, then he did begin to get worried. He got the car out and he and Claire drove to Warwick.

It was about quarter to midnight when they arrived. They saw Jack's car parked, as usual, in the drive, its front almost touching the garage doors; a light was on upstairs, but to Alan's surprise the front door was locked. He told police that Jack never, but never, locked the door when he was in the house. Alan opened the door with his own key, and the first sight that greeted him was that of his father's legs blocking up the tiny hallway. Indeed, it was only with some difficulty that he and Claire managed to get themselves into the house, and they gazed horrified upon a scene of devastation and carnage.

Jack Taylor lay dead in a pool of his own blood, his battered head upon the blood-soaked carpet. Near to her master lay the little brown and white collie mongrel, Tia, dead, with blood all over her face and muzzle. Blood was splashed up the walls, the hall was littered with tools from an old toolbox and everywhere there was birdseed, coated in blood. The brown paper sack that had contained the seed was there too, soaked in blood, Jack Taylor's blood.

The house had been well and truly turned over, with papers tossed around and drawers pulled out and upturned, but the only thing that seemed to be missing was Jack's old leather wallet, darkened with use and age and held together by a rubber band. Alan told police that his father always carried money in this wallet; he liked to carry money. Despite all advice, Jack loved the feel of a fat wallet with a roll of notes. The wallet also contained Doreen's photograph and Jack's driving licence. Alan noted too that there was a hammer missing from the old toolbox usually kept inside the hall cupboard.

Police swung into action and a full scale murder enquiry was soon underway. As far as the investigating officers were concerned, this one was described as 'a Scenes of Crimes Officers' dream', for the murderers had left clues everywhere. 'Might as well have left their names and addresses,' one of the detectives said, and within a matter of hours the men were run to earth and arrested. This was the first time that Warwickshire police used the new technology that enabled them to make a video of the scene of the crime.

Jack Taylor had been stabbed to death with an old kitchen knife, but not before he had been battered by more than twenty hammer blows to his head and shoulders. The killers seemed to have attacked in a frenzy, but Jack Taylor, despite his age and a mild heart condition, had put up a good fight, for there were bruises and cuts on his hands and arms, described by the pathologist as 'defence wounds' received in his attempts to withstand the assault.

The little dog, Tia, also died of stab wounds, and she had been killed before her master, since her dog hairs adhered to the knife which had been withdrawn and plunged into Jack Taylor's body. Her hairs were found around the knife wound in Jack's chest. According to Alan, Tia was a good watchdog, and there can be little doubt she was killed in order to silence her.

Among the scattered tools on the hall floor were two pieces of metal, disc shaped, and a sticky label bearing the legend 'Harrison Domestic Services'. Upstairs, in the bedroom, where papers had been pulled out of various drawers and flung about, police found a receipt for repairs to a washing machine, carried out by Harrison Domestic Services.

A neighbour told police she had chatted to Jack on the morning of Thursday 14th; another neighbour said she had seen him in his greenhouse later that day; a third neighbour said she had noticed a van pull up outside Jack's house as it was turning dusk. Two men got out of the van; they looked like workmen and carried a toolbox. She could not describe the van very fully. The street light had come on and it had distorted the colour.

Harrison Domestic Services turned out to be a perfectly respectable and reputable firm, run by a Mr Neville Harrison, who was easily able to confirm he had sent one of his men to repair Jack Taylor's washing machine, some seven months earlier, on 15th February to be exact. Mr Taylor had paid cash for the repair and Mr Harrison confirmed he always instructed his workmen to put a sticker on any piece of domestic apparatus they repaired. The sticker gave his firm's name and number, so that should further service be required, this information was immediately visible. Advertisement really; all his men carried a quantity with them in their toolboxes.

Mr Harrison identified the disc shaped pieces of metal as parts from a dishwasher. Jack Taylor did not have a dishwasher, but it was highly likely that these bits would have been in the toolbox of anyone whose job it was to service domestic appliances.

Mr Harrison told police he had sent a man called Peter Martin to repair Jack Taylor's washing machine. Martin was self employed and an excellent worker, but after a few weeks he simply disappeared; he had not turned up for work and Harrison had not seen him again.

It took police no time at all to locate Martin and his friend Donald James MacDonald, both with prison records and both together after teaming up while serving sentences in Stafford gaol.

They were now both living at 75 Kings Road, Erdington in Birmingham, a house owned by one Arthur Simpson, a small-time builder, who lived with his common-law wife on the ground floor. Outside, in the street, stood a van, and inside the van a toolbox and a quantity of bloodstained bird seed.

Neither Martin nor MacDonald gave any trouble. As soon as they saw the police officers, Martin said, 'It's been like a nightmare. We didn't mean to go so far. . . He just went mad, and he wouldn't stop. . .'

In the rooms that the two men occupied, police found a cardboard box with a bloodstained hammer and knife; they also discovered Jack's wallet with the photograph of his dead wife, his car log book and his driving licence. MacDonald's boots fitted the bloodstained bootprints found in Taylor's house, and Martin had dog bites on his left hand which corresponded exactly with the teeth of the little dead mongrel, Tia.

All the items removed from the rooms in Kings Road had traces of bird seed, a mixture of four different kinds which Jack used to have made up especially for him, and which he bought in large paper sacks, to feed his much loved and prized canaries.

Robert Peter Martin was adopted into the Martin family in 1950 when he was two years old. His mother is believed to have been a Land Army girl working in Hatton, Warwickshire but after the child was adopted, nothing more was heard of her. Peter Martin seemed to get on well with his adoptive parents and with his older brother, also an adopted child. All went well until 1963 when he got into trouble. He was convicted of taking a car and, with others, attempting to break into a house. He was sent to prison for three years in November 1969, for arson, and it was there he met MacDonald, also serving three years for robbery.

MacDonald came from Pitlochry in Scotland, and had been discharged from the Navy for 'discreditable conduct'. In his case, it seemed to mean constant fighting! He drank, and when in drink became quarrelsome and violent. He married, and there were three daughters of the marriage, but the family ran first an off-licence, then a public house and then a wine bar. Because of MacDonald's excessive drinking, none of these worked out and it is believed it was this that ended the marriage.

Both Martin and MacDonald made a full confession. They told the police that they worked on building sites, but that they spent money as fast as they earned it and were absolutely 'skint'. On 14th November, they were out in the van looking for something that would get them off the building sites for the winter. They had been driving towards Coventry, with no money at all between them and not even enough petrol to get them home again, when Martin recalled servicing the washing machine at 100 Stratford Road in Warwick, and he also remembered the rumours about the owner keeping money by him because he 'didn't believe in banks'. They set out with the intention of threatening Jack Taylor and making him give them some money.

Jack Taylor opened the door to their knock. They told him they had come to repair the washing machine and he said, 'It isn't broken, and I did not send for you. . .'

They hit out at him with the toolbox they carried, he fell back into the hall and they followed him into the house. Taylor then got up and grabbed his own toolbox from the hall cupboard. According to their evidence he put up far more of a fight than they had bargained for, so they panicked and hit him with his own hammer, then stabbed him with the old knife Martin had used in his former employment for stripping off electric cable.

The dog was barking and squealing and wouldn't stop, they said. Martin grabbed it by the muzzle in an attempt to make it shut up, and this is how he came to get his hand bitten. Then he held the dog while MacDonald stabbed it in the neck.

'The place was swimming in blood,' said MacDonald in his statement. 'We sat down on the stairs, and we were both crying. . .'.

'Then we searched the house to make it look as if it had been turned over. We grabbed some clothing and gave things a bit of a wipe.' They took Jack's wallet which contained about a hundred pounds and, after pulling his dead body away from the front door, they left the house. They bought petrol with the stolen money and headed back home, where they bathed, washed their clothing and then went out to get drunk, according to MacDonald. He said he dropped the roll of notes while he was in the pub, trying to get himself drunk, but the money was never found.

MacDonald admitted under questioning that Jack Taylor had recognised Martin as the washing machine repair man and, had he lived, he would have been able to tell police who it was that robbed him.

'The bird seed got everywhere,' he said. 'It stuck to us, in our hair, our clothes. . .'

What Martin and MacDonald did not know and could not have known was that in an old tin in the garage Jack Taylor kept most of his hoard, something like £3,500 in notes. In an elephant's foot, standing in the hallway where they left his murdered body, was a further £100.

Both men stood trial in Birmingham in April 1975 and both got life sentences.

Within a matter of days, police had taken nine hundred statements, checked and cross checked them, dealt with forensic evidence, found the murderers and arrested them, and brought all to a neat conclusion. Like they said, it was 'a Scenes of Crimes Officers' dream'.

What happened to the Great Gun of Rugby?

They still tell the story in Rugby, those old enough to recall some of it, although it is to be supposed that eventually there will be nobody who can remember anything of this event.

It is a bit of a mystery, because the gun has not been seen since, not for more than eighty years.

At the end of the Great War, the war that was supposed to end all wars, in November 1918, battle-weary servicemen, those that had managed to survive, were demobilised very quickly. Cynics told each other it was to avoid having to keep on paying them, and there may have been an element of truth in that. With nobody else left to fight, the War Office discovered it owned quite a lot of hardware, lying around all over the place, and it did not have the slightest idea what it was going to do with it.

Somebody, and we do not know who, which is perhaps just as well, had the very bright idea of donating an item or two to local authorities; to towns and cities where the inhabitants had worked hard for the war effort. Rugby had done a very great deal in this respect. It was a modest town of modest means and modest size, but plainly the townsfolk were patriotic to a man. It had raised in excess of £800,000 in war loans for a start, and had thrown itself heart and soul into doing whatever it could to help. Therefore, it was with some justifiable pride that the Chairman of the Rugby Urban District Council learned from the Army authorities that the town had been allocated a gun 'in recognition of the war effort by the people of Rugby of all classes'.

The gun, a German 4.5 field cannon, was at Warwick

temporarily and it was hoped they would be able to bring it to Rugby as soon as possible. The Council discussed this at length and wondered where on earth they were going to put the gun. Where would be suitable? Where would be appropriate? After much debate, it was decided that the gun – which was due to be delivered on 12th December 1918 – should stand in front of the public baths.

The Council thought they should give the gun some sort of civic reception! This seemed an appropriate response, although they didn't want to do too much. It was too soon after the horrors of the war, and 'too much' could be considered insensitive.

The 12th December wasn't a good day. It was wet and chilly with the odd burst of watery sun. But, despite all, quite a good crowd had gathered to witness the arrival of the gun. And they waited. And they waited, and waited. A messenger eventually arrived with the news that the lorry carrying the gun had broken down at Bilton, some three miles or so off, and another messenger had perforce been despatched to Warwick to collect spare parts.

Well, it was no good just standing there waiting, so the entire crowd decided to march to Bilton to greet the gun. The road in those days was not as it is now; it was only part made up and for most its length it was a sea of mud, particularly in a wet December. But off they all went, the civic dignitaries, led by the Rugby School Corps of Officer Cadets and their band. They met the gun. There were a couple of speeches, they all shook hands and then turned around and marched the three miles back to the town.

The gun was well received when it finally arrived. The site upon which it was destined to stand had been bedecked with bunting and a few Union Jacks waved. The Chairman of the Council, a trifle damp, took his stance beside the gun and addressed the crowd, telling them it was a German gun, captured by the 'gallant boys of the Royal Warwickshire Regiment', and calling for three hearty cheers, readily forthcoming.

The day was, all in all, a memorable occasion for the town of Rugby. This was now *their* gun, for hadn't they earned it?

Within three weeks, the gun was gone. The Army claimed it

back, and it was never seen by anybody in Rugby again.

Four months later, the Army said to the Town Council, 'Would you like a tank instead. . .?' This offer was debated at length at the next meeting and quite a few members were exceedingly sceptical. Many still entertained vague hopes they would get the gun back at some time. The Army reassured them the tank was NOT in lieu of the gun, but was an entirely separate gift.

One or two councillors didn't especially want the tank, and it was suggested that the Chairman should simply write and say 'No thank you'. But in the end, as is the way of all democratic decisions, it was put to the vote – and the 'ayes' won. One or two people muttered they hoped it would not involve another three mile march in the rain! It was decided to put the tank near the Recreation Ground and leave the site of the gun, near the public baths, free just in case they ever got it back.

The tank arrived by rail, complete and in good order, except that its gun had been removed. Having seen service in France, it

The tank given to the town of Rugby in recognition of their part in the war effort was sited near the Recreation Ground.

was scarred by bullet holes. It travelled happily under its own power to its chosen site and was formally handed over by the Officer Commanding.

It was discovered that the tank was a female one. This relates apparently to the number and type of guns with which they were kitted out. Thus, this tank was officially named by the Chairman of the Council 'Cecilia' in honour of the Countess of Denbigh. This good lady had, despite ill health, thrown herself heart and soul into the war effort. She was seriously ill and unable to attend the ceremony, and died in fact two days later.

The tank was eventually enclosed in iron railings 'to prevent access by children' although one or two said it was unnecessary expense since children were hardly likely to run off with it.

So the tank named Cecilia remained there, in front of the rather nice memorial gates to the town's Recreation Ground. Not especially a thing of beauty perhaps, a battle-scarred tank, but Rugby got used to it; the community had earned it and it belonged.

That is until May 1940 when 'they' had it back again. More war effort. The memorial gates, railings and the tank itself were all cut into pieces in the drive for scrap metal, and with them went every inch of the town's lovely ornamental railings. Soon Rugby no longer had a tank named Cecilia – any more than it had its memorial gun . . .

EXPLOSION AT STRATFORD-UPON-AVON

Sometimes you get years that simply aren't good, and 1912 was one of those. A series of depressing events, one following on another. In January came the news that Scott and his party had reached the South Pole only to find they had been pipped at the post by the Norwegian Amundsen; in March it was learnt that the whole expedition had perished almost within sight of safety. In April the wonderful, new, prestigious, romantic and unsinkable liner *Titanic* sank, with appalling loss of life. And then there was a Great British Coal strike. Townsfolk of Stratford-upon-Avon read about all this in their newspapers, went about their daily affairs and tut-tutted, shaking their heads and asking each other 'whatever next?' Little did they know that 'whatever next' was about to happen right in their midst.

On Wednesday, 8th May 1912, about half past eight in the evening, the entire town and the surrounding villages, particularly Alveston and Tiddington, were shaken violently by a terrific explosion and were immediately plunged into what seemed like Stygian darkness. The sky was split asunder by sharp flashes of light and the noise of the explosion reverberated round and round and was heard as far away as Warwick town centre.

It was terrifying. No one knew what was happening. It felt like an earthquake, but Warwickshire is not subject to such forces. It was unrelieved dark everywhere, black as ink, the air filled with smoke and fumes, and particles of something seemed to be showering down from the skies.

People rushed from their dark houses into the equally dark

Members of the Corporation at Stratford-upon-Avon Gasworks after the explosion of 1912.

streets, cannoning into one another in their fear and haste. One elderly gentleman, placidly riding along Birmingham Road in the direction of the town, was abruptly jolted out of his reverie when, with less than half a mile to go, the heavens above him were illuminated with blue streaks and the tremors of the explosion assailed his ears. As for his horse, poor creature, the animal bolted in sheer terror, galloping wildly into the town, ears flattened to the immediate peril of the townsfolk thronging the streets in bewilderment. Only with difficulty was the creature eventually brought to a quivering standstill.

The explosion appeared to emanate from the Birmingham Road direction, and thus the mass of people with one accord turned towards it; towards the town's gasworks. The air remained black and thick and the route was littered with debris. Bits of tiles still seemed to be coming from somewhere and heads were but narrowly missed.

The police arrived and made some attempt to prevent the

crowd getting too dangerously close. The fire brigade came too, and this in itself was no easy task. Within the town limits at this time, it was usual for the men to pull the fire appliance themselves. The Stratford brigade used the horses stabled at the Shakespeare Hotel, but there were problems if the horses were already out, perhaps fetching guests or luggage from the railway station. But they turned up, with their steamer ready to pump for dear life. It was decided, however, that it should not be used, and another ripple of fear ran through the crowd at the mention of escaping gas.

The manager of the gasworks, Mr Job Cranmer, was in his adjoining house when the explosion rent the air. He had eaten his supper and was relaxing with the newspaper when his house – and every other house in the town – was plunged into darkness. He rushed outside as he above all others was mindful of the fact that there were four men working on the night shift in the gasworks and he feared for their safety.

He found crowds of people arriving and being joined by more and more. He could not answer their questions at this time, but he was relieved to see two of his men come staggering out of the darkness towards him. 'Thank God,' he said as he satisfied himself that they were both safe and uninjured, although very shaken. But what about the other two men, Arthur Timms and George Collins? No one had seen them.

The yards all round the works were full of fallen masonry, but upon hearing that two men had not been accounted for, the crowd immediately stripped off coats and set to, heaving stones out of the way, delving deep in their search for the two missing men. A whole troop of Scouts turned up and they too pitched in, but one youngster got hit on the head with a brick and had to be taken to hospital. It was a minor wound, though, and he was not detained.

The firemen, unable to help with their steamer in the usual way, also joined in the search for Timms and Collins. Job Cranmer was getting very upset and agitated; he was the manager and these were his men. What had happened and was he likely to find them dead or injured? He was himself shifting debris when suddenly he shouted to the crowd to be silent, to stand still. They listened, straining their ears, and they heard the sound of the most pitiful groaning. There was a rush to the spot from whence the groans came and willing hands scrabbled frantically, until beneath the piles of broken tiles and bricks, the stoker, Arthur Timms, was revealed. He presented a ghastly and bloody spectacle and was drifting in and out of consciousness. Gentle hands lifted the poor man and carried him to the waiting ambulance, which took him to hospital. His first thoughts were for his workmate, though, for every time he surfaced he kept on asking 'Where's George? Have you got George. . .?'

The search commenced anew. Minutes passed, and a sharp eye in the crowd spotted a fragment of corduroy cloth. More digging at that spot revealed the dead and mangled body of George Collins.

By this time poisonous fumes were being leaked; the gas holder had split and there was a very real fear that the gas could ignite. Arthur Timms made it to hospital – just. He died at midnight.

There was an inquiry, of course. Two men had lost their lives and it was vital to find out *how* they had died and what had caused the explosion that killed them.

Mrs Eliza Timms, wife of Arthur Timms, confirmed his age as 44 and said they lived at Waterloo Cottages on Banbury Road, Stratford-upon-Avon. Yes, she had been with her husband when he died. She had known this would happen, having had a premonition. She had not waited to be called, but in the evening, as soon as she heard the noise, she simply went to the hospital, 'by my own inclination' as she put it. She had known she would find her husband there and it seems as if she had known she would be witnessing his death.

Collins' wife, Annie Eliza, said her husband had been 43. They lived at Tiddington and George Collins had worked at the gasworks for 15 years, albeit with some gaps in his service.

Both wives, now widows, told the inquiry that their husbands had complained about being pushed and the work getting harder. Eliza Timms said that before setting off for work on that fateful evening, her husband had muttered he wished he did not have to go, he dreaded it. She hadn't known what he was referring to really.

Job Cranmer was questioned in his turn. He said that Arthur Timms was of 'blameless' character and had worked for him for a long time. George Collins was not so blameless though. He had been forced to discharge him upon more than one occasion, he said rather sorrowfully.

'Why was this?' he was asked.

'Drunkenness,' he replied. 'But,' he added, 'there was not a better workman when he was sober.'

'Then why did you take him on again?'

'Pressure from outside,' said Mr Cranmer. 'I was asked to give him another chance and I did so. Several times.'

'Do you think he might have had anything to do with the cause of the explosion?'

'I would rather not say.'

In response to a further question, Mr Cranmer said he considered it very unlikely that a spark likely to ignite gas could have been made by metal studs on the soles of any boots. And he said no matches had been discovered. He was warned by the Coroner to keep anything that might be found amid the debris.

The foreman, John Henry Bigg, was new to his job and said he had been trying to get a 'bigger make of gas'. This had, he admitted, caused much unpleasantness and grumbling among the men. On the 8th May, he had looked all around, just as he always did before leaving work and going home, and at that time, all had been well. He had seen Collins and he had been stone cold sober; he had not been drinking.

The inquiry was postponed so that experts could be asked for their opinion and it reopened one week later. The experts had been very thorough and had gone into absolutely everything. Their report to the inquiry was detailed, technical and lengthy, but what it all boiled down to was that they had not found out what had caused the explosion. Their exact summing up was: 'Gas must have leaked from a water overflow, but what caused it to ignite remains a mystery.'

Poor Arthur Timms, the man of blameless character and poor George Collins, who liked a drink at times even at the expense of his job, were decently buried. The members of the inquest jury who had sat through hours of evidence for several days agreed unanimously to hand over their fees to the two widows and their children.

Local councillors visited the site en masse; there was nothing they could say or do really as they dutifully picked their way over and around the rubble that had caused the deaths of two of their constituents. It was all a bit of a mystery – and now few people if any remember where the old gasworks was, for nothing at all remains.

THE LEIGH INHERITANCE

Charles Griffin, a solicitor in Leamington Spa, took on the might of the Law which he himself served, and the might of the Leigh family, in the middle of the 19th century, and deservedly came off worst! Griffin was well known for his involvement in Chartism, the movement of the working classes demanding more political power for themselves, and his own often publicly expressed anti-aristocracy views were no secret either.

Griffin was perfectly entitled to hold whatever views he liked of course; but he allowed these to spill over, blight his professional credibility, obsess him and ultimately destroy him. His campaign of envy and malice towards Chandos, Lord Leigh of Stoneleigh, based upon a pack of not very clever lies, could not prevail and eventually in 1849 Charles Griffin, in the vernacular phrase, got his cum-uppance. It took quite a while, though, for the man was like a terrier with a rat, and would not let go.

In 1786 Edward Leigh of Stoneleigh had died, unmarried, childless and, poor man, a lunatic. His two elder brothers and one younger brother had all died before him, and his estates were inherited by his sisters, the Hon Mary Leigh, and Mrs Ann Hackett. Mary did not marry, and Mrs Hackett died a childless widow. At the time there were no male kindred of poor Edward, and the Hon Mary who died in 1806, bequeathed the property to James Henry Leigh, the head of the Addlestrop branch of the family.

The Leighs were prolific, with branches, seats, titles and lands in many places. Edward was the last of his particular line.

We then come to a certain George Leigh of Lancaster who had

Stoneleigh Abbey (County Record Office – Ref PH 352/171/27)

read in the newspapers all about the Leigh inheritance and the Leigh family. George Leigh decided he was of this self same family, descended from the same stock as Edward, and had, therefore, a perfectly legitimate claim to the inheritance. Thus did he set the ball rolling and the lengthy, expensive and extraordinary charade began.

Anyone, but anyone, may have felt a twinge of envy of the Leighs and their superb seat at Stoneleigh; once upon a time a Cistercian monastery, where around 1714 the celebrated architect, Francis Smith of Warwick, did some of his best – some say his very best – work. The Leighs were total Royalists, to a man. They had refrained from attending divine service at Stoneleigh church in the middle of the 18th century because in so doing they must needs offer prayers for the Hanoverian King, whilst their sympathies and loyalties were one hundred per cent with the Stuarts. So, they built themselves their own chapel. It is believed that Prince Charles Edward, the Young Pretender, or Bonnie Prince Charlie if you prefer it, was a secret visitor to the Abbey.

Another regular visitor, but not in secret, was novelist Jane Austen for her mother was of the Leigh family.

George Leigh made his official claim to the Leigh inheritance in 1813, causing great legal consternation. Just about this time too, Jane Austen published *Pride and Prejudice* and *Mansfield Park*, both of them anonymously.

George Leigh's claim was thoroughly investigated. These things take a long time, and are by their very nature incredibly cumbersome. The evidence was put before the House of Lords, who debated it endlessly, and their findings were published in 1828, and subsequently published in two large volumes of a very tedious nature.

In a nutshell, George Leigh's claim hinged upon a first marriage of one Christopher Leigh who died in 1672. George claimed there had once been a memorial tablet upon a wall in Stoneleigh church, which set this out plainly. It is supposed to have read thus:

Sacred to the memory of the Honourable Christopher Leigh fourth son of the Right Honourable Thomas, Lord Leigh, and Lady Mary, his wife. He married Penelope Cotton, daughter of St G Cotton, Bart, of Combermere Abbey, Cheshire, by whom he had issue Mary, Catherine, Roger and Ferdinand.

He married secondly Constance Clent, daughter of Sir John Clent Esqr of the Borough of Warwick by whom he had issue Thomas.

Roger Leigh of Haigh Hall, eldest son of the above Honourable Christopher Leigh, he married Margaret Higham eldest daughter of James Higham, Esqr of Wigan, Lancashire, by whom he had issue Robert and James.

This memorial slab was evidence of the marriage between Christopher Leigh and Penelope Cotton in the 17th century, and it is from this marriage, and issue, that George claimed descent.

In evidence he trotted out quite a few, probably hand-picked, people from Stoneleigh, who said they recalled this particular memorial slab. They had all seen it regularly when they attended church, or Sunday school, or something of the like. Others called by the other side, declared they recollected nothing like that at all.

Some said the stone had been taken down when repairs were carried out to the church; others recalled seeing Lady Mary Leigh going down into the cellar, followed by workmen bearing a heavy object wrapped in a piece of old carpet.

The marriage is supposed to have taken place at Wrenbury, Cheshire, but the registers for that place were found to have been 'mutilated'. At the same time, the registers for Stoneleigh had pages missing. Inexplicably!

George further suggested that Christopher Leigh's second wife, Constance Clent, suppressed or destroyed her late husband's will and other documents in order that her own son, her one and only child Thomas, could inherit.

In short, a great many somewhat outrageous statements were made, mostly unsubstantiated. The Lords debated long and hard, and in the end dismissed George's claim.

James Henry Leigh was free to continue to enjoy Stoneleigh, and his son, Chandos Leigh, came into possession of it in 1839. All seemed set fair, but this pleasant lull was soon to end.

On 27th October 1844, Lord Leigh and his family were away from home for a few days, and in their absence they had left the Abbey in the capable hands of George Jones, their own solicitor; a man they trusted absolutely and who had always served them well. He was to do so again now.

In the late afternoon of that day George Jones heard men approaching the Abbey gates. It was not to his ears a friendly sound, more purposeful, and so he ordered the gates to be closed and locked. There was something of an altercation when the group of men were refused admission but they were persuaded to leave. George Jones knew well, though, that he had not seen the last of them.

Jones spent a hectic weekend. He obtained the services of several police officers to reinforce the Abbey staff, and all were given instructions about what to do should the 'enemy' return as Jones knew they would. And they did! On the following Monday, and this time the small aggressive group had swollen into a mob, armed with sticks and cudgels.

The ringleader was one James Leigh, a relative of the unsuccessful claimant, George. Jones attempted to reason with him, but realised he was wasting his breath. James told Jones that he (Jones) had no right to be at the Abbey, and without further ado the mob burst in, yelling and shouting, and simply took over the Abbey. Police and staff, heavily outnumbered, received cuts, bruises and knocks on the head.

Confusion reigned supreme, and under cover of it, George Jones hot-footed it to Leamington to obtain assistance. Twenty special constables and six officers marched rapidly upon the Abbey. Jones was with them and quite a few public spirited local people were gathered en route, the latter mostly joining in out of curiosity, thinking they might be in for a bit of entertainment.

By this time the marauders had barricaded themselves into the Abbey, but after a fairly half-hearted fight were persuaded to emerge. They were taken prisoner and charged with a variety of offences: rioting, breaking in, causing damage, assault and so on. It was at this point in the story that Charles Griffin appeared on the scene. As a solicitor, he was slightly involved in the defence of some of the 'followers' whilst James Leigh elected to conduct his own defence.

Leigh admitted there had been some violence, but blamed the police for causing this. (It seems the police were to be made scapegoats then, as they frequently are now. Nothing changes much!)

When he was ordered to 'be quiet' he retorted he had been quiet for the last 30 years, ever since his family had been robbed of their rightful inheritance.

Ultimately, the magistrates were fairly lenient with the followers, but when it came to James Leigh they decided he was entirely to blame and he was sentenced to 18 months' hard labour in prison.

All this was meat and drink to Charles Griffin. He was intrigued to think that Lord Leigh was enjoying an estate and title to which he had no right; one that should belong to poor James Leigh, whose family were obviously the true heirs. He turned James into a sort of folk hero, doing what he had to do to claim what was his own!

Chartism had died down a bit now, and Griffin had time to spare. He spent it amassing information about the Leigh family throughout the generations. In fact, he became totally obsessed with it.

He wrote a little book, a 'slim volume' entitled *Stoneleigh – Thirty Four Years Ago*, and in it he detailed all the evidence he had collected. His allegations were totally astounding. Had it been sold as a work of imaginative fiction, he might have had good sales, but the author was insistent that it was all true, all fact.

He trotted out once more the previously heard stories about the removal of the memorial slab in Stoneleigh church, adding statements from persons who swore they had seen fragments of this slab being built into the cellar wall. He decided that the registers at Wrenbury had been maliciously tampered with by someone pouring chemicals all over the pages. Further evidence in the form of letters had once been available at Combermere Abbey, he insisted, but these too had been stealthily destroyed by someone, the same person who had deliberately torn pages out of the Stoneleigh registers.

In 1814, Lord Leigh had decided to build a bridge across the river. Griffin recounted that at the building of this bridge, some 30 men, mostly itinerant workers, had been murdered, and their bodies buried in many places, including the stonework buttresses of this infamous bridge. These were supposed, according to Griffin, to have been killed because they knew what the Leigh family had been up to, knew who had removed the memorial, knew who had mutilated the parish registers.

The methods used to kill them had been many and varied. Innovative too! Some had been shot by gamekeepers upon Lord Leigh's orders; one or two had been poisoned; one had the distinction of being dropped into a large boiler inside the Abbey itself. Knives had featured: two or three had had large lumps of stone dropped upon their heads from a great height. All this with the absolute connivance of Lord Leigh and his family, and all to ensure they kept quiet about the memorial tablet. Bodies were buried all over the estate.

In May 1848, Griffin made formal application for a warrant to search the Stoneleigh Abbey estate for the bodies of these men. He regaled magistrates with the information he had amassed. He also declared that nine coffin plates had gone missing. Now he, Griffin, was especially anxious to excavate the bridge, for he was convinced it was the last resting place of at least four men.

Lord Leigh vehemently opposed the granting of such a warrant. He said he had nothing to hide. If Griffin demolished the bridge, he would find nothing. Then, not satisfied, Griffin would demand to be allowed to continue with further excavation, demolition, and still nothing would be found, but he, Lord Leigh, would end up with much damage to rectify. Fortunately, magistrates listened, and dismissed Griffin's application.

Such a foolish man was Griffin. Instead of leaving things alone, he had to go further. This move was the straw that broke the camel's back. Lord Leigh must have had the patience of a saint to put up with all this rubbish, but he did win in the end.

The next thing Griffin did was to formally charge Lord Leigh with murder. One supposes Griffin decided he must have aided and abetted his father, James, and others of the family way back when the bridge was built. Griffin produced several witnesses! One, Barnett by name, declared he had seen men disappear as mortar began to set. He said he had seen blood oozing from the bridge abutments; he added that he had seen bodies wrapped in bits of carpet, bodies inside sacks, and he believed these to have been buried in the foundations of this bridge, taken there by the family, after midnight.

He was a good story-teller, and plausible with it. He ended up saying that he had himself fled from Stoneleigh to save his life.Then it was found he was not entirely the innocent man he seemed. He had served prison sentences and was known to be on the very best and friendliest of terms with James Leigh. Immediately he stepped from the witness box, he was re-arrested and charged with perjury, among other things!

The court once more dismissed Griffin's preposterous charge. This time, however, Lord Leigh had had enough; quite enough, and he charged the startled Griffin with libel.

Early in 1849, Warwick Court was once more filled to capacity with all those eager to hear the next chapter in this continuing saga.

Lord Leigh was treated sympathetically. They had all heard Griffin before, but they listened again, and after due care and proper consideration, found him guilty. He was sentenced to two years' imprisonment, with hard labour. He was to find £500 surety, and a further £250 to guarantee his good behaviour upon his eventual release.

Griffin was devastated. He whimpered and wept, and declared he did not have access to such funds. But this cut no ice with the Judge, who curtly told him he should have considered the possible consequences of his actions before he deliberately embarked upon a malicious campaign against Lord Leigh.

* * * *

POSTSCRIPT: One of Griffin's wild allegations does hold a germ of truth – perhaps the only one in the entire farrago. The registers of Stoneleigh are not complete, and there are pages missing. Those covering the years of the Civil War have either gone, or are illegible. This is not all that unusual, for the responsibility rested with the vicar, rector, or clerk in each parish, and possibly there was just too much to-ing and fro-ing at such time.

Shortly after Griffin's antics, the Stoneleigh registers were once more called upon, only this time nothing much was really at stake. It happened thus.

Not a lot remains of the church at Kings Newnham, near Stoneleigh, save the tower. The church wall is part of a farmyard, and the yard itself is where was once the churchyard. At some time in the late 1850s, Lord John Scott, a kinsman of the Leigh family and living at Kings Newnham, held a shooting party. There was good sport; it was a happy and convivial occasion. Then came an unexpected downpour, really heavy rain, and it was suggested they should all repair to the Hall for lunch. En route it was noted that the farmyard was already flooded. After a short break, the guests emerged to find the farmyard dry as a bone. How could this have happened in so short a time? Someone noticed the last trickle of water disappearing into a tiny hole in the corner.

Lord John sent for a couple of his workmen, and had them open the hole. The astonished party found themselves gazing into a rain-filled vault, with coffins floating towards them. The coffins were lifted and the local blacksmith carefully rolled back the lead.

All contained Leighs! One was Francis, Lord Chichester, buried 1653; another contained the body of Sir John Anderson, a son of Lady Chichester by her first husband. In Lady Chichester's coffin there was just a skeleton, but with masses of rich auburn hair.

Lady Audrey Leigh had been a renowned beauty in her day, and in her coffin (she was buried in 1640) she appeared just as beautiful as she ever had been. She looked young, as young as 16 some said. Plump, rosy, with dark eyelashes fanning her cheeks. She was dressed in fine linen, trimmed with five point lace, her white and delicate little hands were piously folded, and in her ears were tiny black earrings in the form of serpents.

It was the last coffin of all to be opened that caused the most consternation. It contained the well preserved body of a young man, and a young, very handsome man, at that, with a neatly trimmed peaked beard. His long brown hair curled slightly upon his shoulders and was dappled with what was later found to be blood. He wore grave clothes of the finest white linen, with the initials 'TB' embroidered in black silk by a skilful hand. His body was covered with sweet herbs, and around his neck was a broad band of black velvet ribbon. It was only when this was touched it was discovered he had been beheaded.

Loving hands had put his head back into place upon his shoulders. Perhaps the same loving hands had dressed him thus for burial, embroidered his linen and, before committing his coffin to the ground, had covered his body with sweet herbs. But who was he? And who was it that had loved him enough?

We do not know the answer, but it is thought – merely an educated guess on the part of those more knowledgeable than myself – that it could be one Thomas Brierley, another kinsman of the Leighs. All the Leighs were Royalist, loyal to King Charles I, and Thomas and his brother, John Brierley, were officers in the King's army. It is known they fled to escape the Roundheads, probably after the defeat at Naseby, just over the border in Northamptonshire. They may have headed towards their nearest kinsfolk at Kings Newnham, or even nearby Stoneleigh. John went to earth at some point and lived to tell the tale, but became separated from his brother who was, so it seems, captured. Nothing more is known about Thomas, and it is by no means certain that this young man was indeed he!

I hasten to add that Lord John Scott caused the vault to be repaired, the coffins to be made good and all to be as it was before. And he saw to it that these bodies, his distant kinsfolk, were properly and reverently re-interred.

DOROTHEA ALLEN'S ESTATE

Sutton-under-Brailes is a delightful, perhaps even picture book, Warwickshire village, on the fringe of the Cotswolds, with all (well perhaps not quite all) the houses fronting onto a truly magnificent village green, once embellished by what was called the 'Warwickshire weed' – the elm. The Great Elm, a local landmark, beneath which generations had frolicked happily, was 150 ft in height and had a girth of some 192 inches. Sadly, you will not need to be reminded of the ultimate fate of these glorious giants when the dread Dutch elm disease arrived in this county around 1970.

The green, thankfully, remains, as lush and verdant as ever. And facing the green, the gates of Sutton-under-Brailes manor, a superb example of a 17th century house, set amid 25 acres or so of garden and grounds. Here for some 60 years lived the mysterious Mrs Dorothea Allen; and here in this lovely house she died in January 1990.

Then indeed, the mystery deepened, for it seems that Mrs Allen had been a very wealthy lady and had deliberately set about disguising her identity, and her past. She left no will, nor did anyone appear to know anything at all about a possible next of kin. But, as you may well imagine, as soon as the news of her accumulated fortune hit the front pages of the newspapers, some three hundred or so vociferous claimants emerged from nowhere.

It was found that Mrs Allen had destroyed family papers, family letters, had sliced the heads off family photographs, and had mutilated her passport, without altogether destroying it. This gave her maiden name as 'Farquharson' but no place of birth. Her vaccination certificate was unearthed, and this gave her date of birth as January 1901, making her 89 when she died, but here again no place of birth was given. It is believed, although by no means certain, that Mrs Allen was educated abroad, in a convent somewhere in Belgium.

The trail was blurred further when it was found there was no way of tracing the marriage of Dorothea and her husband, Captain Robert Eric Allen. Indeed, were they married at all? There is a remote possibility that they married in Connecticut, USA but if this was the case Captain Allen had not actually obtained a divorce from his first wife. Officially, his first marriage was never ended.

The Treasury Solicitors's office began to attempt to find out who Dorothea Allen really was, and if there were any real claimants for a share in her fortune of millions.

Friends and neighbours said Mrs Allen never referred to her family, to her childhood days, or to her education. Or indeed to anything at all in her past. Somehow or other, it was hinted that she had German connections.

Captain Eric Allen came from Sheffield, and in 1927 he and Dorothea founded a company, Spencer Corsets Ltd, in Banbury, using money Dorothea had inherited from her father, who had been involved in one or two property deals. Spencer Corsets Ltd progressed, flourished and eventually joined up with a company in America.

In 1931, the Allens bought the manor of Sutton-under-Brailes and immediately hired the finest designers of that period to restore the 300 year old, 28 roomed house to its former glories. Well, perhaps even more than 'former glories'. The decorations were lavish, and the rooms were furnished with superb pieces. There were seven individually designed bathrooms, one of which was reserved exclusively for Dorothea's dog! The house and all the assets were found to be in Dorothea's name.

And assets there were aplenty, for Dorothea and her Captain lived a most enviable and stylish life. They had a yacht called *Mandoo* and this was moored at St Philip in Barbados, where they owned another estate, smaller this time, just around twelve acres.

The mysterious Dorothea and her husband enjoying a holiday in the Bahamas.

For their many visits to London, they maintained a flat in Kensington; and for visits to New York, they had a luxury flat on Fifth Avenue. Visits to New York were frequent, particularly after their amalgamation with an American company. They had many friends in America and lived quite a hectic life there, with Hollywood stars – among them Clark Gable and Errol Flynn – seated at their dining table.

Their trips to America were always on the *Queen Mary*, First Class, dining at the Captain's table and enjoying all that this superb liner had to offer such travellers.

Mr and Mrs Allen had no children, but on the outbreak of the war in 1939, Dorothea opened their home at Sutton-under-Brailes for evacuees, quite a few of them, and she treated them almost as if they were her own, or at least as if they were related to her. In the extensive grounds around the manor, she built a summer house for them, and they called it 'Snow White's Cottage'. She even had notepaper specially printed for them, with the address 'Snow White's Cottage', so they would be encouraged to write home often to their parents, left behind to suffer the London bombs. The children had a donkey as a pet, but when the creature became a little too elderly to sustain their combined weight, Dorothea got a pony and trap, and in this they could all bowl around the village.

The Captain and Mrs Allen contributed largely to the war effort in many different ways. At about this time, they together designed a body belt or corset for airmen, pilots and crew, worn to offset the effects of 'G-forces' when flying at high speed. Dorothea also organised a Spitfire Fund among their workpeople, persuaded the American side of the business to donate as well and then made up the deficit from her own personal fortune, and was able to present a Spitfire to the RAF at a time when it was desperately needed.

The Captain bought stirrup pumps and ensured that every household in the village had one and was able to use it in the event of fire. Dorothea equipped the village with an ambulance.

The Captain was awarded an OBE in 1957 for his services to industry, and he died in 1965.

There are many conflicting reports about Dorothea. That she and her Captain were happy and worked well together there can be no doubt. Her help during the war years, her use of some of her personal fortune, her thought for the village and her care for the evacuee children indicated that she was a kind and loving woman. And yet, there are reports that she was cold and manipulating, although very attractive, and that she had quite a few lovers both before and after the death of the Captain.

When Dorothea died, her estate came under the care of the Treasury Solicitor until all could be thoroughly investigated. The first thing they discovered was that Dorothea had changed her name no less than three times. And no one was any nearer to finding out who she really was or where she came from. Obviously, this was the way she wanted it and how she had planned it, but why. . .?

The prestigious firm of Sotheby's was given the task of organising the sale of paintings, vintage cars, furniture and so forth. This took place at the manor in Sutton-under-Brailes on 4th September 1990. Dorothea's personal jewellery and small pieces, including items from Cartier and Fabergé – were sold at Sotheby's in Geneva later that year.

Crowds turned up on 4th September. The curious and curiouser, as well as serious buyers. But at the eleventh hour there was a little panic when a letter was received from a German pensioner, Herr Wilfred Kluber, claiming he was Dorothea's heir; he declared that his grandmother was sister to Mrs Allen, both sharing the name Farquharson, and that both were born in Berlin, Dorothea in January 1901. This claim was not thought to be too far-fetched, since it was believed that Dorothea's father was German. Herr Kluber in his seventies, and with a bad heart, could not be at the sale.

Another surprise on this day was the unheralded appearance of a Mrs Muriel Keyte from Torquay. Mrs Keyte said she was the daughter of the Captain – Robert Eric Allen. Her mother and Eric Allen were married at Sheffield on the outbreak of the First World War. He went out to India, came back a Captain, and immediately walked out on his wife and their small daughter, Muriel, but never bothered to go through the business of a divorce. Mrs Keyte, far from resentful, seemed to regard the entire affair with some amusement. She had been traced by a London genealogist who was kept busy trying to unravel Dorothea's origins. Mrs Kyte was not a claimant, had no thought of such a thing, since she was no blood relative of Dorothea and her father, Eric Allen, had died 25 years previously.

The sale exceeded expectations, even the expectations of Sotheby's. The bidding began with around 800 people crowded outside the marquee, unable to get in. A lifetime's collection of luxury went under the hammer, to strangers, and everything fetched more than anticipated. A 1972 Rolls Royce Corniche fetched £66,000; a chrome plated Raleigh bicycle which had once been made exclusively for Dorothea was knocked down for £550. It seems Dorothea had fallen off it and it had never been ridden since. Even a small four-piece egg and cruet set, thought to be worth around £80, was snapped up at £450! In total, the sale at the house raised more than £600,000. The house itself was due to be auctioned later and was expected to fetch in the region of £700,000. With the proceeds of the sale in Geneva added to this, Dorothea had indeed been wealthy. The claimants multiplied.

The office of the Treasury Solicitor is on record as saying they hoped to get it sorted out quickly, and 'get this lot off our books'. They said they had already received 'hate mail'.

Then, in November 1994, Gloria Hunniford hosted the BBC programme *Good Fortune* and, during a live broadcast, sprang a surprise upon a member of the audience, Mrs Susan O'Hagan, telling her that the BBC had solved the mystery of Dorothea Allen's estate and that she, Susan O'Hagan, was likely, as heir, to come in for a large slice of the fortune. She was told she was a second cousin twice removed of the mysterious Dorothea, but Mrs O'Hagan knew nothing of this; she had made no claim at all. Even had this relationship eventually been confirmed by the Treasury Solicitor, it seems Mrs O'Hagan would still have to share with a whole host of others.

In January 1996 it was widely reported that DNA technology had been resorted to in an attempt to solve this now desperate riddle, with the help of a single grey hair from the hairbrush allegedly used by Dorothea. Someone then cautiously said it was first necessary to discover how the single grey hair had come to light! The Treasury publicly said they could run no risk of wrongly allocating the money, for to do so would open the flood gates to costly litigation.

Meantime, researcher Mr Ken Jarrett, from Woodbridge in Suffolk, had also been beavering away to try to find the real Dorothea. And he did. His findings were revealed in the *Mail on Sunday* on 14th January 1996. Mr Jarrett found that Dorothea had been born 101 years previously, in a terrace house in Wadsley Bridge, Ecclesfield, near Sheffield. A wartime pilot had recognised her in the many press photographs and said that she had been his childhood sweetheart and that her name was Dora Brammer.

The claimants were sorted out, probably with some sighs of relief from the authorities. One of Dorothea's (or Dora's) elderly cousins, Basil Whitham from Sheffield, was named her nearest relative in Treasury documents. He and others would each receive something in the region of £20,000 each.

The Treasury Solicitor's office told me this entire investigation had been a headache and had taken a long time to finalise. They confirmed there had been a great many beneficiaries, but declined to be more exact. They also said they had not found out why Dorothea desired to turn herself into an enigma, why she had attempted to so thoroughly disguise herself. They found enough to bring the matter to a satisfactory conclusion, and the papers were now archived but still nobody knows or perhaps *knew* the real Dorothea.

Thus ends the mysterious saga of Dorothea. She and her Captain, whether they were ever married or not, enjoyed a most luxurious lifestyle, 'high on the hoof' as their American colleagues might say. They played in the most famous playgrounds of the world, accumulated wealth, and lived surrounded by beautiful things. But it had to come to a grand finale as always. And as Dorothea approached her own grand finale, she deliberately sought to deceive, to confuse, to cover her tracks and cause everybody a bit of trouble. And wherever she is now, I suspect she is laughing at how very well she succeeded.

ACKNOWLEDGEMENTS

I acknowledge with gratitude the generous help I have received from the following:

City of Birmingham Central Library
City of Coventry Central Library
Coal Mining Authority, Mining Records
Duke of Wellington's Regimental Museum, Halifax
Imperial War Museum
Leamington Spa Library
Nuneaton & Bedworth Main Library
Oxford Cultural Studies, Central Library
Rugby Library
Shakespeare Birthplace Trust Record Office
Stratford-upon-Avon Library
University of Birmingham
Warwickshire County Record Office
Warwickshire Police Authority

BIBLIOGRAPHY

Birtley, Jack *The Tragedy of Randolph Turpin* (New English Library 1975)

Bolitho, Paul *Ripples from Warwickshire's Past* and *More Ripples from Warwickshire's Past* (Private Publications 1992 and 1997)

Burgess, Alan *Seven Men at Daybreak* (London 1960)

Burman, John *Gleanings from Warwickshire History* (Cornish Bros 1933)

Burman, John *Old Warwickshire Families and Houses* (Cornish Bros 1934)

Cave, Lyndon F. *Warwickshire Villages* (Robert Hale 1976)

Coventry Evening Telegraph (pub) *Ghosts and Legends* (1994)

Fogg, Nicholas *Stratford-upon-Avon. Portrait of a Town* (Phillimore 1986)

Griffin, Charles *Stoneleigh – Thirty-four Years Ago* (Private Publication)

Long, Jenny and Barber, Andrew (Eds) *Graciously Pleased* (Mayneset 1988)

Macdonald, Callum *The Killing of Obergruppenfuhrer Reinhard Heydrich* (Macmillan 1989)

McInnes, Peter *Randy. The Final and Complete Biography of Randolph Turpin* (Caestus 1996)

Sutherland, Graham *Dastardly Deeds in Victorian Warwickshire* (Brewin Books 1999)

West, Nigel *Secret War* (Hodder & Stoughton 1992)

Young, Peter *Edgehill 1642* (The Roundwood Press 1967)

Also many Warwickshire pamphlets and various publications of Local Historical Research Groups and the following newspapers:

Birmingham Evening Mail
Coventry Evening Telegraph
Daily Express
Daily Mail
Daily Mirror
Daily Telegraph
Leamington Spa Courier
Mail on Sunday
Stratford upon Avon Herald
The Oxford Mail
And, of course, many old newspapers, now, alas, long defunct.